THE EMPATH AND THE NARCISSIST:

Unmasking Narcissism, Breaking the Cycle, and Healing from Its Impact

Dedication

To those who have felt lost in the storm of narcissistic abuse, questioning their worth and reality, this book is for you. May it serve as a guiding light on your path to healing, clarity, and strength.

To the empaths who give endlessly, love deeply, and often suffer in silence, may you find the courage to set boundaries and reclaim your power.

And to those with NPD who seek understanding, growth, and change, may this book offer insight and a path toward self-awareness and healthier relationships.

This is for all who are ready to break the cycle, heal from its impact, and step into a future of peace and self-empowerment.

Table of Contents

Introduction: Understanding the Structure of This Book

SECTION1 /INTRO
   I. A Captivating Start: The Empath and Narcissist Dynamic
   II. Defining Narcissistic Personality Disorder (NPD)
   III. Origins of Narcissistic Personality Disorder (NPD)
   IV. DSM-5 Criteria and the Spectrum of Narcissistic Behaviors
   V. Understanding Empathy
   VI. Cognitive, Affective, and Compassionate Empathy
   VII. The Strengths and Vulnerabilities of Empaths
   VIII. The Attraction
   IX. Why Empaths and Narcissists Are Drawn Together
   X. The "Love Bombing" Phase
   XI. Purpose and Scope of the Book

SECTION 2

Part I: Understanding Narcissism

Chapter 1: What Is Narcissistic Personality Disorder?
- Definition, Symptoms, and Diagnostic Criteria
- Differentiating Healthy Narcissism from NPD

Chapter 2: The Roots and Causes of Narcissism
- Genetics, Environment, and Upbringing
- How These Factors Contribute to Narcissistic Traits

Chapter 3: The Narcissist's Mindset
- Grandiosity, Entitlement, and the Need for Constant Validation

- The "False Self" Versus the "True Self"
- Fear of Vulnerability

Chapter 4: Types and Tactics of Narcissists
- Overt vs. Covert, Malignant, Somatic, and Cerebral Narcissists
- Common Tactics:
- Gaslighting, Manipulation, Projection, Triangulation, Hoovering, Silent Treatment, and Emotional Abuse

Chapter 5: The Cycle of Narcissistic Abuse
- The Stages: Idealization, Devaluation, and Discard
- How the Cycle Perpetuates Itself

Part II: The Empath's Experience

Chapter 6: The Empath's Profile
- Key Traits and Characteristics
- Strengths and Vulnerabilities in Relationships

Chapter 7: The Toxic Dance: Empath and Narcissist Dynamics
- The Initial Connection and "Love Bombing"
- Why Empaths Are Drawn to Fix and Heal
- How Narcissists Exploit Empathic Tendencies

Chapter 8: Emotional Impact and Recognizing the Red Flags
- Psychological and Emotional Toll: Anxiety, Depression, PTSD, and Low Self-Esteem
- A Checklist for Identifying Narcissistic Patterns
- Trusting Your Intuition

Part III: Breaking the Cycle and Healing

Chapter 9: Setting Boundaries and Establishing Detachment
- The Importance of Boundaries
- Practical Strategies for Boundary Setting
- When and How to Use No Contact or Grey Rock Techniques

Chapter 10: Embracing Self-Care and Self-Compassion
- Mindfulness, Meditation, and Healing Practices
- Cultivating Self-Compassion and Forgiveness

Chapter 11: Seeking Therapy and Building Support
- Finding a Therapist Specialized in Narcissistic Abuse
- Utilizing Support Groups and Additional Resources

Chapter 12: Rebuilding Self-Worth and Moving Forward
- Rediscovering Identity and Passions
- Forming Healthy Relationships
- Tips for a Future Free from Narcissistic Cycles

Conclusion
- Recap of Key Takeaways
- Words of Hope and Encouragement
- concluding Thoughts on Breaking the Cycle of Narcissistic Abuse
- Additional Resources and Further Reading

Appendices
- Glossary of Terms
- Exercises and Journaling Prompts
- Comprehensive Resource List

Introduction: Understanding the Structure of This Book

Healing from narcissistic abuse is not just about recognizing the signs—it's about understanding both the psychology of narcissism and the empath's journey toward recovery. That's why this book is divided into two distinct sections, each serving a crucial role in your path to clarity, self-discovery, and healing.

By structuring the book this way, I aim to provide a comprehensive, balanced, and insightful approach that allows readers to not only recognize the patterns of narcissistic relationships but also equip themselves with the tools to break free and thrive.

Section 1: The Foundation of Understanding

The first section lays the groundwork for everything you need to know about narcissistic personality disorder (NPD) and empathy. It's crucial to understand the dynamics between empaths and narcissists before diving into personal healing.

This section includes:

- A deep dive into narcissistic personality disorder, including its origins, DSM-5 criteria, and the spectrum of narcissistic behaviors.
- The science of empathy—what makes empaths unique, their strengths, vulnerabilities, and why they are often drawn to narcissists.
- The toxic cycle of attraction—how narcissists manipulate through love bombing, devaluation, and discard.

In essence, Section 1 is about education—giving you the knowledge to recognize the patterns and understand both yourself and the narcissist in your life.

Section 2: Breaking the Cycle and Healing

The second section shifts from understanding to action and transformation. It is divided into three parts, each designed to guide you toward breaking free and reclaiming your life.

Part I: Understanding Narcissism

This part focuses on the mindset of a narcissist, the root causes of narcissistic behavior, and the different types of narcissists.

You will learn about common tactics of manipulation, including gaslighting, triangulation, and emotional abuse, so you can recognize and counter them.

Part II: The Empath's Experience

Here, we explore the psychological and emotional toll of narcissistic relationships.

You'll gain insight into why empaths get caught in these toxic dynamics and how to start recognizing red flags before it's too late.

Part III: Breaking Free and Healing

This part is entirely solution-focused, providing actionable strategies for setting boundaries, detaching emotionally, and beginning the healing process.

You'll learn about self-care, therapy, rebuilding self-worth, and forming healthy relationships after narcissistic abuse.

Why This Book is Structured in Two Sections

This book isn't just about understanding narcissists—it's about healing from them. That's why I divided it into these two sections:

1. First, we uncover the truth—how narcissists operate and why empaths are affected.
2. Then, we focus on healing—how to break free, rebuild, and thrive.

By the time you reach the end of this book, you will not only understand the toxic cycle but also have the tools to break it and move forward with confidence and strength.

Now, let's begin.

SECTION 1

I. A Captivating Start: The Empath and Narcissist Dynamic

The Inevitable Pull

There is an almost magnetic force that draws empaths and narcissists together. It is a connection that feels fated, as if two puzzle pieces have locked into place. The empath, with their boundless compassion and deep emotional sensitivity, is drawn to the narcissist's charm and confidence. The narcissist, with their need for admiration and validation, is irresistibly attracted to the empath's giving nature. From the outside, it may seem like an ideal match—one person willing to give and another eager to receive. But beneath the surface, this dynamic is anything but balanced.

At first, the connection feels exhilarating. The narcissist showers the empath with attention, admiration, and grand gestures of affection. They make the empath feel special, as if they have finally found someone who understands them on a soul-deep level. This is often referred to as the "love bombing" phase, where the narcissist puts on a facade of perfection, mirroring the empath's dreams and desires. The empath, eager to believe in the depth of this connection, absorbs the affection like a parched plant soaking up rain.

But the storm is coming. Slowly, almost imperceptibly, the dynamic begins to shift. The praise and admiration from the narcissist turn into subtle criticisms. The warmth is replaced with cold detachment. The person who once made the empath feel cherished now makes them feel inadequate, confused, and desperate to regain the love that once seemed so abundant. The empath, unwilling to accept that the relationship is toxic, doubles down on their efforts to heal, fix, and prove their worth. This is the very cycle that traps so many in relationships with narcissists— the endless chase for a love that never truly existed in the first place.

The Empath's Role

Empaths are natural healers. They have a heightened ability to feel and understand the emotions of others, often to the point of absorbing pain that is not theirs to carry. Their compassion is limitless, and they see potential in people that others may overlook. While this makes them incredible friends, partners, and caregivers, it also makes them vulnerable to those who would take advantage of their kindness.

The empath does not fall for the narcissist because they are weak or foolish. Quite the opposite—they love deeply, believe in second chances, and are willing to stand by those who are struggling. They see the wounded child beneath the narcissist's grandiosity. They recognize the pain that created the narcissist's need for control and validation. And because they are natural healers, they believe that if they love hard enough, if they understand deeply enough, they can help the narcissist become the person they are meant to be.

But this is the greatest trap of all. The empath does not realize that their love alone cannot fix what someone else refuses to acknowledge. The narcissist does not seek healing; they seek control. They are not looking for a partner; they are looking for a source of validation. And no matter how much the empath gives, it will never be enough to fill the void inside the narcissist's heart.

The Narcissist's Need for Control

The narcissist's world is built on a fragile illusion of superiority. Beneath their charm and confidence lies an emptiness they cannot bear to face. They rely on external validation to maintain their self-worth, and they see relationships not as partnerships, but as a means to an end. They do not seek connection in the way an empath does. Instead, they seek admiration, power, and unwavering attention.

To the narcissist, the empath is a perfect source of supply. The empath's kindness, patience, and deep emotional investment provide the narcissist with a steady stream of validation. The narcissist tests the limits of this kindness, pushing boundaries to see how much the empath will endure.

And because the empath wants to believe in the goodness of people, they often tolerate far more than they should.

But the narcissist does not just crave admiration—they also crave control. They thrive on keeping the empath in a constant state of uncertainty. One moment they are loving and attentive, the next they are cold and distant. This unpredictability creates emotional dependency, as the empath becomes desperate to win back the narcissist's affection. The more the empath invests in the relationship, the harder it becomes to walk away.

The Breaking Point

At some point, the empath will reach a breaking point. The weight of the manipulation, the gaslighting, and the constant self-doubt will become too heavy to bear. They will realize that they are giving everything and receiving nothing in return. They will start to see the patterns—the cycle of abuse, the emotional games, the constant need to prove their worth to someone who will never truly appreciate them.

This realization is often painful. The empath will grieve—not just for the relationship, but for the illusion they had built around the narcissist. They will mourn the person they thought they had found, the love they believed was real. But in this grief, there is also power. Because once the illusion shatters, the empath can finally see the truth: they were never the problem. Their love was never the problem. They were simply trying to give to someone who was incapable of truly receiving.

Walking away is not easy. The narcissist will try to pull the empath back in, using every tactic in their arsenal—apologies, promises of change, guilt-tripping, and even anger. They will play the victim, making the empath feel responsible for their suffering. But once the empath understands the dynamic for what it is, they can begin to reclaim their power.

Breaking Free and Reclaiming Self-Worth

The journey to healing is not just about leaving the narcissist; it is about rediscovering oneself. The empath must learn that their worth is not tied to how much they can give to another person. They must recognize that love should never be about suffering, proving, or fixing. True love is mutual, respectful, and nurturing.

Healing begins with boundaries. The empath must learn to say no without guilt, to prioritize their own well-being, and to walk away from relationships that drain rather than nourish them. They must surround themselves with people who uplift them, who see their kindness as a gift rather than a weakness.

Therapy, self-reflection, and support groups can be invaluable during this process. The empath must unlearn the belief that love means sacrifice and instead embrace the truth that love should be reciprocal. They must heal the wounds that made them susceptible to the narcissist's manipulation in the first place, recognizing that their desire to help should never come at the cost of their own happiness.

As the empath heals, they will begin to see the relationship for what it truly was—a lesson. A painful, heartbreaking lesson, but one that has the power to transform them into someone stronger, wiser, and more self-assured. They will learn to trust themselves again, to listen to their intuition, and to walk away from red flags instead of justifying them.

A New Beginning

The empath and narcissist dynamic is one of the most complex and emotionally charged relationships that can exist. It is a dance of light and shadow, hope and heartbreak, giving and taking. But it does not have to be a life sentence.

For the empath, there is life beyond the narcissist. There is love beyond manipulation. There is freedom in knowing that they do not have to fix anyone to be worthy of love. There is power in reclaiming their voice, their boundaries, and their sense of self.

For those who have lived through this dynamic, the pain is real, but so is the possibility of healing. The road forward may not be easy, but it is worth taking. Because on the other side of heartbreak lies a love that is pure, honest, and most importantly deserved.

II. Defining Narcissistic Personality Disorder (NPD)

Narcissistic Personality Disorder (NPD) is one of the most misunderstood and misrepresented mental health conditions. It is often associated with mere arrogance, vanity, or selfishness, but in reality, it is a deeply ingrained and complex disorder that affects not only the individual with NPD but also those around them. To truly understand the dynamics between an empath and a narcissist, it is essential to break down what NPD really is, how it manifests, and the different ways it impacts relationships.

What Is Narcissistic Personality Disorder?

At its core, NPD is a personality disorder characterized by a pervasive pattern of grandiosity, a need for admiration, and a lack of empathy. People with NPD have an inflated sense of self-importance and often believe they are superior to others. However, beneath this grandiosity lies deep-seated insecurity and an unstable sense of self-worth, which they compensate for by seeking constant validation and control over those around them.

While narcissistic traits exist on a spectrum, NPD is a clinical diagnosis that goes beyond ordinary selfish behavior. It is a persistent and dysfunctional pattern of thinking, feeling, and behaving that negatively affects relationships, work, and overall well-being.

The American Psychiatric Association defines NPD in the Diagnostic and Statistical Manual of Mental Disorders (DSM-5) using specific criteria. Understanding these criteria can help clarify the difference between a narcissistic personality trait and a diagnosable disorder.

DSM-5 Criteria for NPD

According to the DSM-5, a person must exhibit at least five of the following traits to be diagnosed with NPD:

1. Grandiose Sense of Self-Importance: They exaggerate their achievements and talents and expect to be recognized as superior, even if their accomplishments do not warrant such recognition.
2. Preoccupation with Fantasies of Unlimited Success, Power, or Beauty: They live in a mental world where they are exceptional and destined for greatness, often disregarding reality.
3. Belief in Their Own Uniqueness: They believe they can only be understood by, or should associate with, other special or high-status individuals.
4. Sense of Entitlement: They expect special treatment and compliance from others without reciprocation.
5. Exploitation of Others: They take advantage of people to achieve their own goals, often with no remorse or guilt.
6. Lack of Empathy: They struggle to recognize or care about the feelings and needs of others.
7. Envy of Others or Belief That Others Are Envious of Them: They are either jealous of others' success or assume that others are jealous of them.
8. Arrogant and Haughty Behaviors: They come across as condescending, dismissive, or superior to others.

A diagnosis of NPD is typically made by a mental health professional through extensive evaluation. While many people may exhibit narcissistic traits at times, it is the persistent, rigid, and damaging nature of these traits that defines NPD as a disorder.

The Spectrum of Narcissism

Not all narcissists are the same, and NPD manifests in different ways. Some individuals with narcissistic traits may function relatively well in society, while others engage in highly destructive behaviors. Understanding the spectrum of narcissism can help differentiate between varying degrees of the disorder.

1. Healthy Narcissism: Some level of narcissism is normal and even beneficial. Confidence, ambition, and self-preservation are traits that, when balanced, contribute to success and well-being.

2. Narcissistic Traits: Many people display occasional narcissistic behaviors, such as seeking validation or prioritizing their own needs, without having full-blown NPD.
3. Pathological Narcissism (NPD): When narcissistic traits are extreme, inflexible, and negatively impact relationships, work, and emotional health, they qualify as NPD.
4. Malignant Narcissism: A severe form of NPD that overlaps with antisocial behaviors, aggression, and a complete lack of remorse. Malignant narcissists are often manipulative, deceitful, and even sadistic.

How NPD Develops

The exact causes of NPD are not fully understood, but research suggests a combination of genetic, environmental, and psychological factors contribute to its development.

1. Childhood Experiences: Many individuals with NPD experienced childhood environments that were either excessively critical or excessively indulgent.

Some grew up in households where they were constantly praised, leading them to develop an exaggerated sense of superiority. Others were subjected to neglect, emotional abuse, or unrealistic expectations, leading them to construct a false self as a defense mechanism.

2. Genetic Factors: Studies indicate that personality disorders, including NPD, may have a hereditary component. A family history of narcissistic traits, mood disorders, or other personality disorders can increase the likelihood of developing NPD.
3. Brain Structure and Functioning: Neurological studies suggest that differences in brain structure, particularly in areas related to empathy and emotional regulation, may contribute to NPD.

Common Myths and Misconceptions About NPD

Because the term "narcissist" is frequently used in everyday conversation, many myths and misconceptions about NPD have emerged. Here are some common misunderstandings:

1. "All narcissists are confident and successful."

While some narcissists project an image of success, many are deeply insecure and struggle to maintain their self-worth without external validation.

2. "Narcissists can't feel emotions."

They do experience emotions, but they often suppress vulnerability and struggle with genuine emotional intimacy.

3. "All narcissists are abusive."

While many narcissists engage in manipulation and emotional harm, not all are overtly abusive. Some function in society without causing direct harm to others.

4. "Narcissists can never change."

While personality disorders are deeply ingrained, some individuals with NPD who seek therapy and commit to self-awareness can work on managing their behaviors.

Why Understanding NPD Matters

For those who have been in relationships with narcissists, understanding NPD is crucial to making sense of their experiences. It explains why narcissists behave the way they do, why they seem to lack genuine empathy, and why they create cycles of emotional turmoil.

For individuals who recognize narcissistic traits within themselves, this understanding can be a gateway to self-awareness and potential change. While many narcissists resist therapy, those who are willing to acknowledge their patterns and work on them can develop healthier relationships and coping mechanisms.

For empaths and survivors of narcissistic abuse, this knowledge serves as protection. Recognizing the signs early, understanding the tactics used by narcissists, and learning how to establish firm boundaries can help prevent further emotional harm.

By unmasking the reality of NPD, this book seeks to provide clarity, validation, and empowerment. The next chapter will dive deeper into the origins of NPD—how it develops, what influences it, and how early experiences shape the narcissistic mind. Understanding where narcissism comes from is the first step in breaking free from its impact.

III. Origins of Narcissistic Personality Disorder (NPD)

Understanding where Narcissistic Personality Disorder (NPD) comes from is crucial in comprehending the behaviors and thought patterns of individuals with this condition. While it may be easy to label narcissists as simply selfish or cruel, the reality is far more complex. The development of NPD is influenced by a combination of genetic predispositions, early childhood experiences, and environmental factors. Many narcissists are not born that way—rather, they are shaped by circumstances that reinforce their maladaptive behaviors and coping mechanisms.

This section explores the major contributing factors to NPD, including childhood trauma, dysfunctional family dynamics, and biological influences.

The Role of Childhood Experiences

One of the most significant factors in the development of NPD is early childhood experiences. Research suggests that many individuals with NPD experienced environments in which their emotional needs were either neglected or excessively indulged. These early relationships, particularly with primary caregivers, shape a child's sense of self and their ability to form healthy emotional connections.

1. Emotional Neglect and Conditional Love

Many narcissists were raised in environments where love and acceptance were conditional—given only when they met certain expectations or performed in a way that pleased their caregivers. Instead of being loved for who they were, they learned that love was something they had to earn. This often creates deep emotional wounds and a fragile sense of self-worth.

Example: A child who only received praise when they excelled in academics or sports might learn that their value is tied to achievements rather than their inherent worth.

Long-Term Effect: As an adult, this person may continue to seek validation and admiration from others to maintain a sense of self-worth, leading to the grandiosity and entitlement often seen in narcissists.

2. Overindulgence and Excessive Praise

Conversely, some individuals with NPD were raised in environments where they were excessively praised, indulged, or treated as "special" beyond reason. When parents constantly tell a child they are superior to others and deserve special treatment, the child may develop an inflated self-image.

Example: A child who is never corrected, always praised as "the best," and never taught humility may grow up believing they are inherently better than others.

Long-Term Effect: This sense of entitlement and superiority can manifest in adult narcissists who expect the world to cater to them and struggle with criticism or failure.

3. Abuse and Trauma

Some individuals with NPD come from backgrounds of abuse, neglect, or extreme criticism. In these cases, narcissism becomes a defense mechanism—a way to survive an environment where vulnerability was dangerous.

Example: A child who was constantly criticized, humiliated, or physically abused may develop a grandiose self-image to mask deep feelings of worthlessness.

Long-Term Effect: These individuals may grow up learning to suppress their true emotions and instead create a "false self" that appears confident, successful, and untouchable.

Dysfunctional Family Dynamics

Beyond individual parental behavior, overall family dynamics can also play a significant role in the development of narcissistic traits.

1. Parentification and Role Reversal

In some families, children are forced to take on adult responsibilities, either emotionally or physically. This is known as "parentification," where a child is expected to meet the emotional needs of their parent rather than the other way around.

Example: A child who constantly had to reassure their depressed or narcissistic parent may learn that their needs don't matter.

Long-Term Effect: This can lead to narcissistic traits where the individual either suppresses their emotions entirely or demands constant validation from others.

2. Favoritism and Sibling Rivalry

Children who grow up in households where one child is favored over others may develop narcissistic traits in response to either being the "golden child" or the "scapegoat."

Golden Child: Constant praise and preferential treatment can create an inflated self-image.

Scapegoat: Repeated criticism and blame can lead to defensive narcissism, where the individual later compensates with grandiosity.

3. Emotionally Unavailable Parents

When parents are emotionally distant, children may struggle with developing a strong sense of self-worth. They may learn to suppress their emotions and develop manipulative or controlling behaviors to get their needs met.

Example: A child who is ignored unless they make a dramatic scene may learn that manipulation and attention-seeking are necessary for survival.

The Biological and Genetic Factors

While environment plays a huge role in the development of NPD, biology also contributes.

1. Genetic Predisposition

Studies suggest that personality disorders, including NPD, can have a genetic component. If a parent or grandparent exhibited narcissistic traits, there may be a higher likelihood that a child will develop similar tendencies.

Example: A family history of narcissism, antisocial traits, or other personality disorders may increase the risk of developing NPD.

2. Brain Structure and Functioning

Neurological studies indicate that individuals with NPD may have differences in brain regions responsible for empathy, emotional regulation, and impulse control. Specifically:

Reduced Gray Matter in the Prefrontal Cortex: This area is linked to decision-making, impulse control, and emotional regulation.

Altered Activity in the Amygdala: This part of the brain is associated with processing emotions, particularly fear and empathy.

While these biological differences do not cause NPD on their own, they may contribute to how individuals process emotions and interact with others.

Can Narcissists Change?

One of the biggest questions surrounding NPD is whether individuals with the disorder can change. The answer is complicated. Because NPD is a personality disorder, it is deeply ingrained in an individual's thinking and behavior. However, with the right interventions, some narcissists can develop self-awareness and work toward change.

Barriers to Change

1. Lack of Self-Awareness: Many narcissists do not see anything wrong with their behavior.
2. Fear of Vulnerability: Admitting flaws threatens their fragile self-esteem.
3. Resistance to Therapy: Many narcissists view therapy as unnecessary or beneath them.

What Helps?

- Intensive Therapy: Approaches like Cognitive Behavioral Therapy (CBT) and Dialectical Behavioral Therapy (DBT) can help narcissists develop emotional regulation and self-awareness.
- Motivation for Change: Some narcissists seek help when their relationships or careers suffer due to their behavior.
- Accountability: Being held accountable for their actions—either by life circumstances or those around them—can sometimes lead to change.

Conclusion to section

The development of NPD is a complex interplay of genetics, environment, and learned behaviors. It is not simply a choice but rather the result of deep-seated survival mechanisms formed in response to childhood experiences. Understanding these origins helps us approach narcissism with both awareness and clarity.

For those who have suffered narcissistic abuse, recognizing these patterns does not excuse harmful behavior but provides insight into why narcissists act the way they do. Knowledge is power, and understanding the roots of NPD can help survivors break free from its cycle.

In the next chapter, we will explore the different types of narcissists and how they manifest in relationships. While all narcissists share common traits, there are key variations that shape how they interact with others—and how they inflict harm.

IV. DSM-5 Criteria and the Spectrum of Narcissistic Behaviors

Understanding Narcissistic Personality Disorder (NPD) begins with examining the diagnostic criteria outlined in the Diagnostic and Statistical Manual of Mental Disorders, Fifth Edition (DSM-5). This framework, established by mental health professionals, defines NPD as a pervasive pattern of grandiosity, a constant need for admiration, and a lack of empathy that affects relationships, work, and overall functioning. However, narcissism exists on a spectrum, meaning that while some individuals may meet the full criteria for NPD, others may display narcissistic traits without having a diagnosable disorder.

This section will explore:

- The DSM-5 criteria for NPD
- How narcissistic behaviors vary in intensity
- The spectrum of narcissism, from healthy confidence to pathological grandiosity

The DSM-5 Criteria for Narcissistic Personality Disorder (NPD)

According to the DSM-5, for an individual to be diagnosed with NPD, they must exhibit at least five of the following nine criteria:

1. Grandiose Sense of Self-Importance
   - Exaggerates achievements and talents
   - Expects to be recognized as superior without commensurate accomplishments
   - Example: A person who constantly brags about their success and demands admiration without actual proof of their superiority
2. Preoccupation with Fantasies of Unlimited Success, Power, Beauty, or Ideal Love
   - Often daydreams about being the most powerful, intelligent, or desirable person

- Believes they deserve only the best, whether in career, romance, or status
3. Belief in Being Special and Unique
   - Feels only "high-status" people or institutions can understand them
   - Example: A narcissist may refuse therapy unless they see a "world-renowned" therapist
4. Excessive Need for Admiration
   - Requires constant validation, praise, and attention
   - Becomes upset when admiration is lacking or insufficient
5. Sense of Entitlement
   - Unreasonable expectations of favorable treatment
   - Believes rules do not apply to them and expects special privileges
6. Interpersonally Exploitative Behavior
   - Takes advantage of others for personal gain
   - Forms relationships based on how others can serve their needs
7. Lack of Empathy
   - Inability to recognize or relate to the feelings and needs of others
   - Dismisses the emotions of those around them, often appearing cold or indifferent
8. Envy of Others or Belief That Others Are Envious of Them
   - Resents others' success while believing people secretly admire or envy them
9. Arrogant and Haughty Behavior or Attitudes
   - Frequently looks down on others, acting as if they are inferior

For a diagnosis, these behaviors must be pervasive, inflexible, and present in multiple aspects of life, such as work, relationships, and social interactions. The disorder must also cause significant distress or impairment in functioning.

Narcissism as a Spectrum

Narcissism exists on a continuum, meaning that not all narcissists meet the criteria for NPD. While some people have a healthy level of narcissism, others exhibit harmful, pathological traits. Understanding this spectrum can help differentiate between normal confidence, high self-esteem, and full-blown NPD.

1. Healthy Narcissism

Not all narcissism is bad. In fact, a certain level of self-importance and confidence is essential for success.

Example: A confident leader who takes pride in their work and achievements without exploiting or demeaning others

Characteristics:

- High self-esteem
- Motivation to achieve
- Ability to accept criticism
- Empathy toward others

2. Narcissistic Traits (Subclinical Narcissism)

Some individuals exhibit narcissistic behaviors without having NPD. They may be self-centered or entitled but still function well in relationships and work.

Example: A person who enjoys being admired but does not manipulate or exploit others

Characteristics:

- Competitive and driven
- May crave validation but still capable of forming meaningful relationships
- Can recognize when they are wrong and adjust behavior

3. Pathological Narcissism (NPD and Beyond)

At the extreme end of the spectrum lies full-blown NPD, where narcissistic behaviors cause significant harm to others.

Example: A person who lies, manipulates, and exploits others without remorse

Characteristics:

- Inability to accept responsibility
- Chronic need for admiration
- Emotional abuse toward partners, friends, or employees

- Often involved in unstable relationships

Important Note: Not everyone who is arrogant or selfish has NPD. The difference lies in severity, consistency, and impact on others.

The Mask of Narcissism

Many narcissists hide their insecurities beneath a carefully crafted exterior. This "mask" allows them to appear charming, confident, and successful, especially in the early stages of relationships or professional settings.

- The "False Self" vs. The "True Self"
- The False Self: The confident, charming, and grandiose persona they present to the world
- The True Self: The deeply insecure, fearful, and often wounded self they keep hidden

Why Narcissists Fear Vulnerability

- Any criticism or rejection threatens to expose their fragile self-esteem
- They lash out or become defensive to avoid confronting their real emotions

This is why narcissists react with rage, gaslighting, or silent treatment when they feel threatened. Their self-worth is built on a fragile foundation that cannot handle genuine introspection.

Conclusion to section

Narcissistic Personality Disorder is more than just arrogance or selfishness—it is a deeply ingrained disorder that affects how a person views themselves and others. By understanding the DSM-5 criteria and the spectrum of narcissistic behaviors, we can better identify narcissistic tendencies in those around us.

For those dealing with a narcissist in their lives, whether a partner, parent, friend, or boss, recognizing where they fall on this spectrum can help in deciding how to navigate the relationship.

In the next chapter, we will explore how different types of narcissists behave and how their traits manifest in personal and professional relationships. Understanding these variations will help in identifying the unique challenges posed by different narcissistic personalities.

V. Understanding Empathy

Empathy is the ability to understand, feel, and share another person's emotions and experiences. It is the glue that holds human relationships together, allowing us to connect on a deep level, offer support, and foster compassion. But empathy is not a singular trait—it exists in different forms and intensities, influencing how individuals perceive and respond to the emotions of others.

For empaths—those who experience heightened sensitivity to the emotions of others—empathy can be both a gift and a curse. It allows for profound connections but also makes them vulnerable to manipulation, particularly in relationships with narcissists.

This section will explore:
- The different types of empathy
- The traits and vulnerabilities of empaths
- The role of empathy in relationships
- How narcissists exploit empathy

The Different Types of Empathy

Empathy is not a one-size-fits-all concept. According to psychologists, there are three main types of empathy:

1. Cognitive Empathy (Understanding Another's Perspective)

Cognitive empathy is the ability to intellectually understand what someone else is feeling without necessarily experiencing the emotion yourself.

Example: A lawyer may use cognitive empathy to predict how a jury will react to an argument, but this doesn't mean they emotionally feel the same way as the jurors.

Strengths: Helps in communication, conflict resolution, and leadership.

Potential Downsides: Can be used manipulatively—many narcissists have high cognitive empathy but lack emotional empathy, which allows them to read others' emotions without actually caring.

2. Emotional Empathy (Feeling What Others Feel)

Emotional empathy occurs when a person physically and emotionally feels what someone else is experiencing.

Example: Seeing someone cry can make an emotionally empathetic person tear up or feel a tightness in their chest.

Strengths: Creates deep emotional bonds, fosters kindness, and promotes social harmony.

Potential Downsides: Can lead to emotional exhaustion, boundary issues, and vulnerability to toxic relationships.

3. Compassionate Empathy (The Drive to Help)

Compassionate empathy goes beyond understanding and feeling emotions—it drives action to help those in distress.

Example: A nurse who not only understands and feels a patient's pain but also actively seeks ways to alleviate their suffering.

Strengths: Encourages meaningful action, problem-solving, and moral responsibility.

Potential Downsides: Can lead to compassion fatigue, where constant caregiving drains emotional energy.

Most healthy individuals have a balance of these three types. However, when one form dominates, it can lead to either emotional detachment or over-identification with others' pain.

What Makes an Empath?

An empath is someone with an exceptionally high level of emotional and compassionate empathy. They don't just understand others' emotions—they absorb them.

Traits of an Empath

- o Highly intuitive: Can sense when something is wrong, even when nothing is said.
- o Emotionally absorbing: Feels the emotions of others as if they were their own.
- o Deeply compassionate: Has an overwhelming urge to help and heal others.
- o Sensitive to energy shifts: Picks up on changes in mood and atmosphere.
- o Dislikes conflict: Feels deeply affected by tension, anger, or negativity.

Empaths experience both the beauty and burden of extreme emotional sensitivity. They can form deep, meaningful relationships, but they can also struggle with setting boundaries—a trait that makes them prime targets for narcissists.

The Strengths and Vulnerabilities of Empaths

Being an empath comes with incredible strengths, but without boundaries, these strengths can turn into weaknesses.

Because empaths struggle to disconnect from others' emotions, they often feel drained, anxious, and emotionally depleted after prolonged exposure to toxic individuals.

VI.   How Narcissists Exploit Empathy

Narcissists lack genuine emotional empathy, but they are often highly skilled at recognizing and manipulating others' empathy. This is how the toxic empath-narcissist dynamic begins.

The Narcissist's Strategy

1. Love Bombing:

The narcissist mirrors the empath's emotions and presents themselves as their perfect match.

The empath feels an intense, soul-level connection.

2. Exploiting Compassion:

Once the empath is emotionally invested, the narcissist begins to demand unconditional support, admiration, and forgiveness.

The empath, believing they can "heal" the narcissist, tolerates the abuse.

3. Gaslighting and Emotional Manipulation:

When the empath expresses concern, the narcissist invalidates their feelings, making them question their own reality.

Example: "You're overreacting. You're too sensitive."

4. Draining the Empath:

Over time, the empath loses their sense of self while constantly trying to soothe the narcissist.

The relationship becomes one-sided, with the empath giving and the narcissist taking.

5. Discard and Repeat:

When the empath is emotionally exhausted, the narcissist may discard them and move on to a new source of validation.

If the empath tries to leave, the narcissist might hoover (attempt to suck them back in with false promises).

Breaking the Cycle: How Empaths Can Protect Themselves

While empathy is a beautiful trait, it must be balanced with self-protection. Here are a few strategies for shielding yourself from emotional manipulation:

1. Recognize Manipulation Early

If someone constantly plays the victim, demands attention, or invalidates your feelings, these are red flags.

Healthy relationships are mutual and reciprocal.

2. Set Firm Boundaries

Saying no is not selfish—it's necessary.

Example: "I care about you, but I cannot take responsibility for your emotions."

3. Detach from Toxic Energy

Spend time in quiet reflection or nature to cleanse yourself from emotional overload.

Meditation, journaling, or engaging in hobbies can help ground you.

4. Prioritize Self-Care

Empaths often put others first, but self-care is not selfish.

Healthy sleep, diet, and exercise help maintain emotional balance.

5. Seek Support

Therapy, support groups, or confiding in a trusted friend can help process emotional wounds.

Learning about narcissistic abuse helps validate your experiences.

Section conclusion

Empathy is one of the most powerful forces in human connection—it allows us to love deeply, offer support, and create meaningful relationships. However, when empathy is unprotected, it can become a liability, leaving individuals vulnerable to manipulation and emotional exhaustion.

For empaths, learning how to balance compassion with self-protection is crucial. Recognizing toxic patterns, setting firm boundaries, and prioritizing self-care can help preserve emotional well-being.

In the next chapter, we will explore the powerful attraction between empaths and narcissists, and why these relationships often turn into cycles of emotional highs and devastating lows.

VII. Cognitive, Affective, and Compassionate Empathy

Empathy is often thought of as a singular ability, but in reality, it exists on a spectrum. The way we connect with others emotionally is shaped by different forms of empathy, each playing a unique role in how we perceive, process, and respond to emotions. The three primary forms of empathy—cognitive, affective, and compassionate empathy—vary in their depth and impact on relationships.

Cognitive empathy is the ability to understand another person's emotions on an intellectual level. It involves recognizing what someone else is feeling without necessarily sharing in that emotion. This type of empathy is useful in professions like therapy, law, or leadership, where understanding another's perspective is crucial, but maintaining emotional detachment is necessary. However, cognitive empathy can also be used in manipulative ways. Many narcissists possess strong cognitive empathy, allowing them to read others' emotions and exploit them for personal gain.

Affective empathy, also known as emotional empathy, is the ability to actually feel what another person is experiencing. When someone cries, an affectively empathetic individual might feel sadness as if it were their own emotion. This type of empathy deepens personal connections and is common among empaths. However, it can also be overwhelming, leading to emotional exhaustion if not managed properly.

Compassionate empathy takes emotional understanding one step further—it drives action. When someone is suffering, compassionate empathy compels a person to help, whether by offering comfort, providing solutions, or simply being present. While this form of empathy is a powerful force for good, it can also lead to burnout, especially when someone continually gives to others without taking time to recharge.

Understanding these different types of empathy is essential for anyone who finds themselves emotionally drained by their interactions with others. For empaths, striking a balance between feeling and protecting their own well-being is key to maintaining healthy relationships.

VIII.   The Strengths and Vulnerabilities of Empaths

Empaths possess an extraordinary ability to connect with others on a deep emotional level. They intuitively sense emotions, even when unspoken, and often prioritize the well-being of those around them. Their ability to see the good in people makes them natural healers, compassionate friends, and supportive partners. However, these same qualities can also make them susceptible to emotional manipulation and exploitation.

One of the greatest strengths of empaths is their intuitive nature. They can sense shifts in energy, pick up on subtle cues, and often know when something is wrong before others do. This makes them excellent at providing emotional support. Additionally, their ability to deeply feel allows them to form strong, meaningful connections with people, making their relationships fulfilling and emotionally rich.

However, the downside of this heightened emotional sensitivity is that empaths often struggle with boundaries. They absorb the emotions of those around them, sometimes to the point of feeling drained or overwhelmed. This makes them particularly vulnerable to toxic individuals, especially narcissists, who seek out emotionally giving people to manipulate.

Another challenge empaths face is their tendency to prioritize others over themselves. They may take on the pain of those they love, believing it's their responsibility to fix or heal them. This self-sacrificing nature, while noble, can lead to emotional depletion and even codependency.

For empaths to thrive, they must learn how to protect their energy. Setting firm boundaries, recognizing manipulation early, and prioritizing self-care are essential for maintaining emotional balance. Empathy is a gift, but without proper safeguards, it can become a source of pain rather than connection.

IX.   The Attraction: Why Empaths and Narcissists Are Drawn Together

The dynamic between empaths and narcissists is one of the most fascinating—and tragic—patterns in human relationships. Despite being polar opposites in emotional capacity, they are often magnetically drawn to one another. But why?

At first, the attraction seems natural. Empaths are healers, deeply compassionate individuals who seek to understand and nurture those around them. Narcissists, on the other hand, crave validation, admiration, and emotional energy from others. To an empath, a narcissist often appears as someone who needs love, someone they can "fix" with enough care and understanding. To a narcissist, an empath is an ideal source of emotional supply, someone who will constantly pour love and attention into them without demanding true reciprocity.

Empaths are naturally giving, while narcissists are naturally taking. This imbalance creates a toxic dependency, where the empath continues to give, hoping to heal or change the narcissist, while the narcissist continues to take, offering only enough affection to keep the empath attached.

Additionally, narcissists have a way of making empaths feel special in the beginning. They often shower their targets with attention and affection, mirroring their desires and creating a sense of deep connection. This manipulation plays on the empath's longing for emotional depth, making them believe they've found someone who truly understands them.

Unfortunately, this attraction often leads to heartbreak. Once the narcissist has secured the empath's devotion, they begin to withdraw affection, manipulate, and devalue them. The empath, believing they can "fix" the situation, works harder to please the narcissist, falling deeper into the cycle of abuse.

Recognizing this dynamic is crucial for empaths who find themselves repeatedly drawn to toxic relationships. Understanding that love should be mutual, not one-sided, is the first step toward breaking the cycle and forming healthier connections.

X. The "Love Bombing" Phase

One of the most deceptive and dangerous tactics used by narcissists is love bombing—a period of excessive attention, affection, and flattery designed to rapidly pull the target into emotional dependency. This phase is intoxicating, making the recipient feel as though they've found the perfect partner, but it is ultimately a form of manipulation.

During the love bombing phase, the narcissist mirrors their target's desires. If an empath values deep emotional conversations, the narcissist will engage in them. If the empath longs for romance, the narcissist will provide grand gestures. The attention feels intense, consuming, and exhilarating, leaving the target believing they've met their soulmate.

The reason love bombing is so effective is that it floods the brain with dopamine—the chemical responsible for pleasure and reward. The relationship becomes addictive, making it difficult for the target to see the warning signs of manipulation.

However, love bombing is not real love. It is a strategy designed to create dependency. Once the narcissist feels secure in their control, they begin to withdraw, becoming distant, critical, or emotionally unavailable. The sudden shift leaves the target confused and desperate to regain the affection they once received. This is how the narcissistic cycle of idealization, devaluation, and discard begins.

Understanding love bombing is key to breaking free from its spell. Real love is consistent, patient, and mutual, not an overwhelming flood of affection followed by emotional starvation. Recognizing the signs early can prevent empaths from being ensnared in this toxic dynamic.

XI. Purpose and Scope of the Book

This book is designed to provide a comprehensive and compassionate exploration of the empath-narcissist dynamic. Whether you are someone who has suffered at the hands of a narcissist, an empath struggling to maintain healthy relationships, or even an individual with narcissistic traits seeking to understand yourself better, this book offers insight, validation, and practical strategies for healing.

- Through psychological research, real-life experiences, and expert advice, this book will:
- Help you understand narcissistic personality disorder and its impact on relationships.
- Provide insight into the mind of an empath, including their strengths and vulnerabilities.
- Examine why narcissists and empaths are drawn to each other and how this dynamic unfolds.
- Offer tools for breaking free from toxic cycles, setting boundaries, and healing from narcissistic abuse.
- Explore the possibility of growth and self-awareness for individuals with narcissistic traits.

At its core, this book is about empowerment. It seeks to help those who have been manipulated reclaim their sense of self, build healthier relationships, and ultimately find peace, strength, and emotional freedom.

SECTION 2

Part I: Understanding Narcissism

What This Section Is About: Understanding Narcissism

Part I of this book lays the foundation for understanding Narcissistic Personality Disorder (NPD) and the behaviors associated with it. Many people use the term "narcissist" casually, but true narcissism goes far beyond arrogance or self-centeredness—it is a complex personality disorder that shapes how individuals think, feel, and interact with others.

This section explores what narcissism really is, from its diagnostic criteria in the DSM-5 to its various forms, including grandiose, covert, and malignant narcissism. It delves into the psychological roots of NPD, examining how childhood experiences, trauma, genetics, and environment contribute to its development.

Understanding narcissism requires looking beyond stereotypes. While narcissists often appear confident, their behaviors are rooted in deep-seated insecurity, shame, and a fragile sense of self-worth. This section explains the internal struggles that drive narcissistic behavior, such as the need for validation, an inability to handle criticism, and the use of manipulation as a defense mechanism.

Additionally, this part of the book breaks down the tactics narcissists use in relationships, including gaslighting, love bombing, projection, and emotional manipulation. These behaviors are designed to control others while protecting the narcissist's fragile ego.

By the end of this section, you will have a clear, in-depth understanding of narcissism, how it manifests, and how it affects those around them. This knowledge is essential whether you are dealing with a narcissist in your personal life, trying to heal from narcissistic abuse, or simply seeking to understand this complex disorder from a psychological perspective.

Chapter 1:
What Is Narcissistic Personality Disorder?

Narcissistic Personality Disorder (NPD) is one of the most misunderstood and widely debated personality disorders. The term "narcissist" is often thrown around to describe anyone who is selfish, arrogant, or self-absorbed, but true NPD goes far beyond these traits. It is a deeply ingrained, complex psychological condition that affects how a person perceives themselves and others. Individuals with NPD often struggle with a distorted self-image, an intense need for validation, a lack of empathy, and difficulties maintaining meaningful relationships.

Understanding NPD is essential—not only for those who have been affected by narcissistic individuals but also for those who may struggle with narcissistic tendencies themselves. This chapter will break down what narcissism truly is, how it is diagnosed, and how it differs from normal self-confidence or ambition.

Definition, Symptoms, and Diagnostic Criteria

Narcissistic Personality Disorder is classified as a Cluster B personality disorder in the DSM-5 (Diagnostic and Statistical Manual of Mental Disorders, Fifth Edition). Cluster B disorders are characterized by dramatic, emotional, and unpredictable behaviors. NPD, in particular, is marked by an exaggerated sense of self-importance, a constant craving for admiration, and a profound lack of empathy for others.

The DSM-5 Criteria for NPD

According to the DSM-5, an individual must exhibit at least five or more of the following traits to be diagnosed with NPD:

1. A Grandiose Sense of Self-Importance – Narcissists believe they are superior to others. They often exaggerate their achievements, expect admiration, and feel entitled to special treatment.
2. Preoccupation with Fantasies of Unlimited Success, Power, Beauty, or Love – They may daydream about being the most powerful, intelligent, or desirable person and believe they deserve recognition for their "special" qualities.
3. Belief That They Are Unique and Can Only Be Understood by Other Special or High-Status People – Narcissists often feel superior and tend to associate only with people they perceive as equally exceptional.
4. Need for Excessive Admiration – Constant validation is required to maintain their fragile self-esteem. Without admiration, they feel unworthy or insecure.
5. A Sense of Entitlement – Narcissists expect special treatment and get frustrated when others don't cater to their needs or desires.
6. Exploitative Behavior – They take advantage of others for personal gain, whether emotionally, financially, or professionally.
7. Lack of Empathy – They struggle to recognize or care about the feelings and needs of others. Their interactions are often transactional, driven by self-interest rather than genuine emotional connection.
8. Envy of Others or Belief That Others Are Envious of Them – Narcissists often compare themselves to others, feeling superior yet simultaneously insecure.
9. Arrogant or Haughty Behavior – They act in a way that suggests they are above others, belittling those they perceive as inferior.

While these traits define NPD, not every narcissist will exhibit all of them. Some may be more overt in their narcissism, displaying grandiosity openly, while others may be covert, masking their narcissistic tendencies with false humility or victimhood.

How NPD Manifests in Daily Life

- NPD doesn't just exist in theory—it profoundly impacts the lives of those who have it and those who interact with them. Individuals with NPD often:

- Struggle with relationships – Their inability to empathize and tendency to manipulate make it difficult for them to form deep, meaningful connections.
- React poorly to criticism – Even mild feedback can trigger intense anger, defensiveness, or silent treatment.
- Seek attention and admiration – They thrive on praise and become distressed when they feel ignored or undervalued.
- Engage in controlling behaviors – Whether in personal or professional settings, they often try to control others to maintain a sense of superiority.
- Use people for their own gain – They may appear charming at first but often reveal a pattern of taking more than they give.

This disorder often leads to high levels of conflict in relationships, workplaces, and families. It is not simply about being "full of oneself"; it is about deeply ingrained patterns of thought and behavior that can be harmful to both the narcissist and those around them.

Differentiating Healthy Narcissism from NPD

Not all narcissism is bad. In fact, healthy narcissism is essential for self-confidence, ambition, and success. The key difference between healthy and pathological narcissism lies in the ability to balance self-interest with empathy, accountability, and emotional regulation.

What Is Healthy Narcissism?

Healthy narcissism is the ability to:

- Have self-confidence without the need to put others down.
- Pursue goals and ambitions while still considering the needs of others.
- Accept criticism and feedback without feeling personally attacked.
- Maintain meaningful relationships without manipulating or exploiting people.

People with healthy narcissism value themselves but do not require constant validation from others. They recognize their strengths and achievements but remain open to learning, growing, and acknowledging their mistakes.

Differentiating Healthy Narcissism from NPD

Narcissism, at its core, is not inherently bad. In fact, some degree of narcissism is essential for self-confidence, personal ambition, and resilience. The difference between healthy narcissism and pathological narcissism (NPD) lies in how these traits are expressed and whether they cause harm to oneself or others.

What Is Healthy Narcissism?

Healthy narcissism is a balanced form of self-esteem that allows individuals to value themselves without feeling superior to others. People with healthy narcissism are confident in their abilities, take pride in their accomplishments, and have a strong sense of self-worth. However, this confidence does not come at the expense of others. They do not manipulate, exploit, or belittle people to feel good about themselves.

Someone with healthy narcissism can accept criticism, acknowledge their mistakes, and continue growing. They can pursue personal success while still maintaining empathy and forming meaningful relationships. Instead of seeking constant validation, they are secure in their self-worth and do not require excessive admiration to function.

For example, a person with healthy narcissism might feel proud of their achievements at work and seek recognition for their efforts. However, they do not react with rage or humiliation when given constructive feedback. Instead, they can take criticism as an opportunity for growth.

What Is Narcissistic Personality Disorder?

In contrast, pathological narcissism, or Narcissistic Personality Disorder, goes beyond self-confidence and becomes a destructive pattern of behavior. Individuals with NPD have an exaggerated sense of self-importance, a deep need for admiration, and a fundamental lack of empathy for others. Their self-worth is fragile, often built on grandiosity and external validation rather than true self-confidence.

Unlike someone with healthy narcissism, a person with NPD cannot handle criticism well. Even minor feedback can feel like a personal attack, triggering defensive reactions such as anger, blame-shifting, or the silent treatment. They may also manipulate, gaslight, or exploit others to maintain their sense of superiority.

A key hallmark of NPD is the inability to form deep, meaningful relationships. While a healthy narcissist can maintain strong friendships and romantic relationships, someone with NPD often struggles with intimacy and connection. Their relationships are frequently transactional, based on what the other person can provide rather than mutual respect and love.

Key Differences Between Healthy Narcissism and NPD

One of the most significant differences between the two is how they respond to criticism. A person with healthy narcissism can handle feedback without feeling personally attacked. They might feel momentarily upset but are capable of processing their emotions and using the feedback constructively. However, someone with NPD may react with extreme defensiveness, rage, or an immediate attempt to discredit the person giving the criticism.

Another major distinction is empathy. A person with healthy narcissism is still capable of understanding and respecting other people's feelings, even if they are confident in their own worth. On the other hand, individuals with NPD struggle to recognize or care about how their actions affect others. They may dismiss others' emotions as unimportant or view vulnerability as a weakness.

Additionally, their sense of entitlement sets them apart. While a healthy narcissist may have ambition and confidence, they do not expect special treatment or believe they are inherently superior to others. In contrast, those with NPD often feel they deserve privileges without putting in effort. They may expect others to cater to their needs without reciprocation.

Finally, emotional regulation plays a crucial role. People with healthy narcissism have the ability to control their emotions, manage stress, and handle setbacks in a mature way. Those with NPD, however, are prone to extreme mood swings, outbursts, and manipulative behaviors when things do not go their way. Their emotional instability often leads to patterns of conflict in personal and professional relationships.

When Does Narcissism Become a Problem?

Narcissism becomes problematic when it begins to interfere with daily life, relationships, and personal growth. Many successful people exhibit traits of narcissism—such as ambition, confidence, and pride—but they can still function well in society and maintain meaningful relationships. However, when narcissism reaches the level of NPD, it damages relationships, impairs emotional well-being, and creates persistent patterns of manipulation and exploitation.

For those who have narcissistic tendencies but do not meet the criteria for full-blown NPD, self-awareness and therapy can be powerful tools for change. Recognizing harmful behaviors and making efforts to develop empathy, accountability, and emotional regulation can prevent narcissistic traits from becoming destructive.

However, individuals with full-blown NPD often resist treatment because they struggle to acknowledge their flaws. They may view therapy as unnecessary or feel that the problem lies with others rather than themselves. This is why NPD can be particularly challenging to treat, requiring specialized therapy approaches that focus on building self-awareness and emotional growth.

Final Thoughts on Differentiating Healthy and Pathological Narcissism

Not all narcissism is bad. Healthy narcissism allows people to have confidence, ambition, and self-respect without harming others. It enables individuals to pursue success while maintaining emotional stability and genuine connections.

On the other hand, Narcissistic Personality Disorder is a deeply ingrained pattern of entitlement, grandiosity, and lack of empathy that disrupts relationships and emotional well-being. It is not just an inflated ego—it is a serious disorder that affects how a person thinks, feels, and interacts with others.

Understanding the difference between healthy and pathological narcissism is essential in recognizing when narcissistic traits become harmful. If narcissistic tendencies start leading to manipulation, exploitation, emotional instability, or difficulty maintaining relationships, it may be a sign of something deeper than just self-confidence. Recognizing these patterns is the first step toward awareness, healing, and growth.

Narcissistic Personality Disorder is not simply about confidence or arrogance—it is a complex condition rooted in deep emotional wounds, insecurities, and maladaptive coping mechanisms. Understanding the difference between healthy and pathological narcissism is crucial in recognizing when narcissistic traits become harmful.

This chapter has provided a foundation for understanding what NPD is, how it manifests, and how it differs from normal self-confidence. The next chapters will explore the origins of narcissism, different types of narcissistic personalities, and the psychological tactics they use to manipulate others.

Whether you are trying to heal from a relationship with a narcissist, recognize these patterns in yourself, or simply gain a deeper understanding of the disorder, this knowledge is a powerful step toward awareness, growth, and healing.

Chapter 2:
The Roots and Causes of Narcissism

Narcissistic Personality Disorder (NPD) and narcissistic traits do not develop in a vacuum. They are shaped by a complex interplay of genetics, environment, and upbringing. While some individuals may be predisposed to narcissism due to biological factors, their experiences and relationships—particularly in childhood—play a crucial role in determining whether those traits develop into a full-blown personality disorder.

This chapter explores the origins of narcissism, looking at the genetic and neurological underpinnings, the impact of childhood experiences, and the environmental influences that contribute to the formation of narcissistic traits.

Genetics and Neurological Factors

Scientific research suggests that narcissism has a genetic component, meaning that certain individuals may be biologically predisposed to developing narcissistic traits. Studies on twins and families indicate that personality traits, including those associated with narcissism, can be inherited. This does not mean that narcissistic traits are directly passed down from parent to child, but rather that some people may be born with temperaments that make them more prone to developing narcissistic tendencies.

Neurological studies have also provided insight into the brain differences observed in individuals with NPD. Research suggests that people with narcissistic traits may have structural and functional abnormalities in the brain regions associated with empathy, emotional regulation, and self-reflection. The prefrontal cortex and the limbic system—specifically the amygdala—are responsible for processing emotions, self-awareness, and social interactions. Some studies indicate that narcissists show reduced activity in the brain areas responsible for empathy and emotional regulation, which may explain their difficulty in understanding or caring about others' emotions.

However, genetics alone cannot determine whether someone will develop narcissistic traits. While a person may be born with a biological predisposition, it is their experiences, upbringing, and social environment that shape how these traits manifest.

The Role of Childhood Environment and Upbringing

A person's early life experiences play a critical role in the development of narcissistic traits. The way a child is raised, how their caregivers interact with them, and the emotional environment they grow up in can all contribute to narcissism.

Excessive Praise and Overvaluation

One pathway to narcissism is excessive parental praise and unrealistic overvaluation. Some children are raised in environments where they are constantly told they are superior to others, exceptional, or deserving of special treatment. While parental encouragement is essential for building confidence, when children are repeatedly told they are "better" than others and should be admired unconditionally, they may develop an inflated sense of self-importance.

Parents who excessively praise their children without teaching them accountability, empathy, or resilience may inadvertently foster grandiosity and entitlement. These children grow up expecting admiration and special treatment, leading to difficulty handling criticism, setbacks, or rejection later in life.

Emotional Neglect and Abuse

On the opposite end of the spectrum, many narcissists do not come from overly praising households but rather from emotionally neglectful or abusive environments. Some children grow up with caregivers who fail to provide emotional warmth, validation, or a sense of security. In response to this neglect, they may develop a defensive and exaggerated self-image as a survival mechanism.

Children who are constantly criticized, ignored, or emotionally abandoned may learn to suppress their true emotions and construct a "false self"—a grandiose and invulnerable persona that shields them from feelings of rejection or worthlessness. This false self becomes their identity, masking their deep-seated insecurities.

In cases of childhood abuse, narcissistic traits can emerge as a way to regain control and protect oneself from vulnerability. If a child experiences verbal, physical, or emotional abuse, they may develop a tough, unempathetic exterior to cope with the pain. As adults, they may continue to seek power and dominance in relationships, mirroring the dynamics they experienced in childhood.

Inconsistent Parenting: Alternating Between Praise and Criticism

Another factor that contributes to the development of narcissism is inconsistent parenting, where a child experiences both excessive praise and intense criticism. In these situations, caregivers may idolize the child at one moment and harshly criticize them the next, creating confusion and insecurity.

This type of upbringing leads the child to develop an unstable sense of self-worth, making them overly dependent on external validation. As a result, they may grow into adults who crave admiration yet fear rejection, constantly seeking approval while simultaneously pushing others away.

Parental Narcissism and Learned Behavior

Children of narcissistic parents are also at a higher risk of developing narcissistic traits. In households where one or both caregivers exhibit narcissistic tendencies, children learn by example. They may be taught—either explicitly or through observation—that dominance, manipulation, and emotional detachment are necessary for survival.

Some children imitate their narcissistic parent's behaviors, adopting the same lack of empathy, entitlement, and need for admiration. Others, however, may reject these traits and become people-pleasers or empaths, developing the opposite characteristics in an effort to avoid becoming like their parents.

How These Factors Contribute to Narcissistic Traits

The combination of genetics, environment, and upbringing influences how narcissistic traits manifest in adulthood. A person who inherits a biological predisposition toward narcissism and is raised in a neglectful or overly indulgent environment is more likely to develop stronger narcissistic traits than someone who grows up in a nurturing and emotionally stable household.

The Need for External Validation

Many narcissists struggle with self-esteem regulation because their sense of self-worth was shaped by inconsistent validation in childhood. If a child only received attention when they achieved something extraordinary, they may grow up believing that love and acceptance are conditional. This leads to a lifelong craving for admiration and external approval, making them hypersensitive to criticism.

Emotional Defenses and Lack of Empathy

Children who were emotionally neglected or abused often learn to suppress their emotions as a form of self-protection. Over time, this emotional suppression leads to a lack of empathy, as they never learned how to process emotions in a healthy way. Instead of forming deep emotional connections, they develop a self-focused, defensive, and manipulative approach to relationships.

Grandiosity as a Coping Mechanism

For some individuals, narcissistic grandiosity is a shield against deep-seated insecurity. If they grew up feeling unloved, insignificant, or inadequate, they may overcompensate by constructing a grandiose self-image. This image allows them to feel superior and untouchable, helping them avoid the painful feelings of rejection they experienced in childhood.

Why Some People Develop NPD While Others Do Not

Not all individuals who experience neglect, overvaluation, or childhood trauma develop NPD. The difference lies in individual resilience, personality, and social influences. Some people may experience the same childhood circumstances but develop healthier coping mechanisms through supportive relationships, self-awareness, or therapy. Others, however, may internalize these experiences in a way that leads to persistent narcissistic patterns.

Final Thoughts on the Roots of Narcissism

The development of narcissistic traits is rarely caused by one single factor. Rather, it is a complex interaction of genetic predisposition, childhood experiences, and environmental influences that shape an individual's personality. While narcissism can be deeply ingrained, understanding its origins provides insight into why narcissists behave the way they do—and, in some cases, how healing and change may be possible.

Recognizing the roots of narcissism also helps survivors of narcissistic abuse understand that narcissists are often shaped by their own painful pasts. While this does not excuse their behavior, it provides perspective on why they struggle with empathy, emotional regulation, and genuine connection.

Chapter 3:
The Narcissist's Mindset

Understanding the mindset of a narcissist is key to comprehending their behaviors, motivations, and emotional struggles. Narcissists operate with a unique psychological framework that revolves around grandiosity, entitlement, and an insatiable need for validation. Beneath this exterior, however, lies a fractured self—what psychologists refer to as the "false self" versus the "true self". This division creates a fragile sense of identity, which in turn fuels a deep-seated fear of vulnerability.

This chapter delves into the core psychological mechanisms that drive narcissistic behavior, helping readers grasp why narcissists act the way they do and why they struggle with self-awareness, empathy, and emotional stability.

Grandiosity, Entitlement, and the Need for Constant Validation

One of the defining characteristics of narcissistic personality disorder is grandiosity, a belief in one's superiority, uniqueness, and importance. This grandiosity often goes hand in hand with entitlement, which is the expectation of special treatment and privileges. Underneath it all, however, lies an insatiable need for validation, as the narcissist's self-worth is entirely dependent on external approval.

The Illusion of Superiority

Narcissists often see themselves as exceptional, unique, and superior to others. This belief may manifest in different ways—some narcissists consider themselves intellectually gifted, others see themselves as physically attractive, and some believe they are morally superior. This grandiose self-image is not just about self-confidence; it is a deep-seated psychological defense mechanism designed to protect them from underlying feelings of inadequacy.

To maintain this illusion, narcissists may:

- Exaggerate their achievements—They may lie about or embellish their successes to appear more accomplished than they are.
- Look down on others—Belittling others helps reinforce their own sense of superiority.
- Surround themselves with admirers—They seek people who feed their ego and validate their self-importance.

The problem with grandiosity is that it is unsustainable. Reality often contradicts the narcissist's inflated self-perception, which leads to narcissistic injury—a profound emotional wound triggered by criticism, failure, or rejection.

Entitlement and Exploitation

Because narcissists believe they are superior, they also feel entitled to special treatment. They expect to be recognized, respected, and accommodated without putting in the same effort as others. This entitlement can manifest in different ways:

- In relationships – They expect unwavering admiration and compliance from partners, family, and friends.
- At work – They believe they deserve promotions, praise, or privileges without necessarily earning them.
- In social situations – They expect others to accommodate their needs, often disregarding boundaries.

Entitlement often leads to exploitation, as narcissists believe they have the right to use others for their own gain. They may manipulate, deceive, or take advantage of people without guilt or remorse, as they lack the capacity to see others as equal individuals with their own needs and emotions.

The Never-Ending Need for Validation

Despite their grandiose exterior, narcissists do not have stable self-esteem. Instead of relying on internal confidence, they depend entirely on external validation to feel good about themselves. This is why they constantly seek praise, attention, and admiration.

If they do not receive enough admiration, they may:

- Fish for compliments by exaggerating their accomplishments.
- Create drama to draw attention back to themselves.
- React aggressively to criticism, even if it is constructive.
- Devalue others to make themselves feel superior.

Their dependence on validation creates a fragile emotional state. If they are criticized or ignored, they may lash out in anger, withdraw completely, or attempt to regain control through manipulation. This never-ending cycle makes it nearly impossible for narcissists to maintain stable relationships, as their emotional needs are insatiable.

The "False Self" Versus the "True Self"

At the core of narcissism lies a profound identity crisis. Narcissists do not operate with a single, cohesive self-image. Instead, they rely on a false self—a grandiose, carefully constructed facade designed to protect their deeply wounded true self.

The Birth of the False Self

The false self begins developing in childhood, often as a response to emotional neglect, overvaluation, or abuse. If a child is constantly told they must be perfect to be loved or if they experience extreme criticism, they learn to suppress their authentic emotions and create a new, more acceptable version of themselves.

This false self serves multiple purposes:

- It protects them from feelings of inadequacy—By constructing a powerful, admired persona, they avoid confronting their hidden insecurities.
- It helps them gain social validation—They create an image that attracts admiration, respect, and attention.
- It allows them to suppress painful emotions—They bury feelings of shame, sadness, or vulnerability beneath their grandiose exterior.

The Hidden True Self

- The true self of a narcissist remains buried, stunted, and underdeveloped. This true self is often characterized by:
- Deep-seated insecurity—Despite their outward confidence, they constantly feel unworthy.
- Shame and self-doubt—They are haunted by feelings of inadequacy they refuse to acknowledge.
- Emotional immaturity—Because their true self was never fully developed, they struggle with emotional regulation.

Narcissists go to great lengths to avoid confronting their true self, as it represents everything they fear: weakness, rejection, and failure. This is why they become defensive, manipulative, and aggressive when their grandiose self-image is threatened.

Why the False Self is Unsustainable

The biggest problem with the false self is that it is a lie. No matter how much admiration and validation they receive, the narcissist knows—on some level—that their self-image is not real.

This is why many narcissists eventually experience emotional breakdowns, identity crises, or deep depression. They can only maintain the illusion for so long before the truth seeps through.

Fear of Vulnerability

Perhaps the most defining characteristic of a narcissist's mindset is their intense fear of vulnerability. Vulnerability means exposing one's emotions, admitting mistakes, and accepting imperfections—all things that narcissists find terrifying.

Why Narcissists Fear Vulnerability

For most people, vulnerability is a necessary part of forming deep, meaningful connections. However, for narcissists, vulnerability feels like a direct threat to their survival. This fear stems from:

- Early childhood wounds—They learned that showing emotions led to rejection or punishment.
- A lack of emotional tools—They never developed the skills to process emotions in a healthy way.
- A rigid self-image—Admitting flaws would shatter their carefully constructed false self.

How Narcissists Avoid Vulnerability

To protect themselves, narcissists engage in defensive behaviors that keep them from feeling exposed. These include:

- Deflection—They shift blame onto others instead of admitting fault.
- Anger and aggression—They lash out when confronted with uncomfortable truths.
- Emotional withdrawal—They disappear or give the silent treatment to avoid dealing with emotions.
- Manipulation—They twist conversations to regain control.

The Consequences of Avoiding Vulnerability

By avoiding vulnerability, narcissists:

- Sabotage relationships—They struggle to form deep emotional bonds.
- Remain emotionally stunted—They never develop true self-awareness or emotional intelligence.
- Experience chronic dissatisfaction—No amount of external validation can fill their internal void.

For those dealing with narcissists, understanding their fear of vulnerability can provide clarity. It explains why they resist accountability, reject intimacy, and react so strongly to criticism. However, it also highlights the difficulties of helping a narcissist change, as true transformation requires facing the very emotions they work so hard to avoid.

Conclusion to chapter

Healing from the effects of narcissistic relationships—whether as a survivor of abuse or as someone with Narcissistic Personality Disorder seeking self-awareness—is a journey, not a single moment of realization. Understanding narcissism is not about assigning blame, but about empowering ourselves with knowledge, boundaries, and self-compassion.

For those who have endured narcissistic abuse, know that your pain is real, but so is your strength. You are not defined by what you have suffered, and healing is possible. It takes time, but with the right support, you can rebuild your self-worth and step into a future free from manipulation and self-doubt.

For individuals who recognize narcissistic traits within themselves, awareness is the first step toward change. No one is doomed to their patterns if they are willing to reflect and grow. Therapy, self-reflection, and accountability can lead to healthier relationships and a more authentic self.

Breaking the cycle of narcissistic dynamics—whether as a survivor or someone working to overcome these tendencies—requires courage. But with that courage comes freedom. You deserve relationships built on mutual respect, love, and understanding. No matter where you are in this journey, know that hope exists, and healing is within reach.

Chapter 4:
Types and Tactics of Narcissists

Understanding the different types of narcissists and their manipulation tactics is essential for recognizing and protecting yourself from harmful dynamics. Narcissistic traits can manifest in a variety of ways, ranging from overt displays of grandiosity to subtle, insidious emotional manipulation. In this chapter, we will explore the different subtypes of narcissists and the psychological tactics they use to maintain control over their victims.

Overt vs. Covert, Malignant, Somatic, and Cerebral Narcissists

Not all narcissists behave in the same way. While they share a core set of traits—such as a need for admiration, lack of empathy, and a fragile self-esteem—these traits can manifest differently based on the individual's personality and coping mechanisms.

Overt Narcissists

Overt narcissists, also known as grandiose narcissists, are the most easily recognizable. They display their narcissism openly and often dominate conversations with their self-importance. They are loud, arrogant, and constantly seek admiration. Overt narcissists often believe they are superior to others and have an exaggerated sense of their own talents, achievements, and intelligence.

They tend to:

- Boast about their successes, real or exaggerated.
- React with anger or aggression when criticized.
- Dismiss or belittle others' feelings.
- Show little concern for the well-being of those around them.
- Because they are so obvious in their narcissism, overt narcissists can be easier to identify, but their manipulations can still be deeply damaging.

Covert Narcissists

Unlike overt narcissists, covert narcissists are more subtle and may even appear shy or self-effacing at first. They crave the same validation and superiority as overt narcissists but go about it in more passive ways.

Covert narcissists often:

- Play the victim to gain sympathy and control.
- Use passive-aggressive tactics rather than direct confrontation.
- Have a fragile self-image masked by self-deprecation.
- Manipulate others through guilt and silent treatment.

Because they appear more sensitive and wounded, covert narcissists can be harder to detect. They use emotional manipulation rather than obvious arrogance, making their abuse more insidious and confusing for their victims.

Malignant Narcissists

Malignant narcissists are the most dangerous type. They not only exhibit the traits of classic narcissism but also have antisocial tendencies, often showing signs of sadism, paranoia, and aggression. Unlike other narcissists who primarily seek admiration, malignant narcissists derive pleasure from controlling, harming, or humiliating others.

They are more likely to:

- Engage in calculated emotional, psychological, or even physical abuse.
- Show no remorse for their actions.
- Lie and manipulate for personal gain.
- Exhibit sociopathic or psychopathic tendencies.

Malignant narcissists are often found in positions of power, where they can exert control over others with little consequence. Relationships with them can be deeply traumatic.

Somatic Narcissists

Somatic narcissists derive their self-worth from their physical appearance and sexual attractiveness. They obsess over their looks, fitness, or sexual conquests, using their bodies as a means to gain admiration and control.

Common traits include:

- Excessive focus on appearance, often seeking cosmetic procedures.
- Constant need for validation about their attractiveness.
- Using sex or seduction as a form of control.
- Devaluing partners once they no longer serve their ego.

Somatic narcissists often cheat or seek out multiple partners to reinforce their desirability. They can be emotionally distant, seeing partners as objects rather than individuals with feelings.

Cerebral Narcissists

Unlike somatic narcissists, cerebral narcissists derive their self-worth from intelligence, knowledge, or professional achievements. They believe they are intellectually superior to others and often belittle those they see as less intelligent.

They tend to:

- Dominate conversations with intellectual jargon.
- Look down on others who do not meet their perceived level of intelligence.
- Avoid emotional intimacy, seeing emotions as weaknesses.
- Seek admiration through academic or career accomplishments.

Cerebral narcissists can be just as manipulative as other types, using their intelligence as a weapon to demean and control others.

Common Tactics of Narcissists

Regardless of their type, narcissists use various psychological tactics to manipulate and control their victims. Understanding these tactics can help individuals recognize unhealthy patterns and protect themselves.

Gaslighting

Gaslighting is a psychological manipulation tactic used to make someone question their own reality. A narcissist will distort facts, deny previous statements, or accuse the victim of being overly sensitive or forgetful to create confusion and self-doubt.

Examples of gaslighting include:
- "That never happened. You're imagining things."
- "You're too emotional; you always overreact."
- "You're crazy. Everyone else agrees with me."

Over time, gaslighting can erode a person's self-trust, making them reliant on the narcissist for validation.

Manipulation

Narcissists use manipulation to maintain power and control over others. They might use charm, deceit, or emotional coercion to get what they want. This often includes love bombing—showering someone with excessive affection early in a relationship to gain trust—only to later withdraw it as a form of punishment.

Projection

Projection is when a narcissist attributes their own negative traits or behaviors to someone else. If they are lying, they will accuse their victim of dishonesty. If they are being unfaithful, they will accuse their partner of cheating. This tactic serves to deflect responsibility and create confusion.

Triangulation

Triangulation occurs when a narcissist pits two people against each other to maintain control. This can happen in romantic relationships, friendships, or family dynamics. The narcissist might:

- Compare their partner to an ex to make them feel insecure.
- Tell a friend that another friend is talking badly about them.
- Use a third party to validate their own perspective while discrediting their victim.

This keeps the victim off balance and dependent on the narcissist for approval.

Hoovering

Named after the vacuum cleaner brand, hoovering is a tactic used to suck a victim back into a toxic relationship. After discarding or devaluing someone, a narcissist may suddenly return with apologies, promises to change, or nostalgic messages meant to rekindle the relationship.

Hoovering can take many forms, such as:

- Sending a "random" text to see if the victim will respond.
- Making promises they never intend to keep.
- Pretending to be in distress to elicit sympathy.

This cycle often repeats, keeping the victim trapped in emotional turmoil.

Silent Treatment

- When a narcissist feels challenged or their control is threatened, they may withdraw completely, giving their victim the silent treatment. This tactic is meant to:
- Punish the victim for perceived wrongs.
- Make the victim feel desperate for the narcissist's attention.
- Reinforce the narcissist's power in the relationship.

Being ignored can be as psychologically damaging as outright verbal abuse, leading victims to feel invisible and unworthy.

Emotional Abuse

Emotional abuse is a core component of narcissistic relationships. This can include:

- Constant criticism and belittling.
- Blaming the victim for the narcissist's own issues.
- Controlling the victim's decisions, relationships, or finances.
- Instilling fear or insecurity to keep the victim dependent.

Unlike physical abuse, emotional abuse leaves no visible scars, making it harder to identify and escape.

Conclusion

Recognizing the different types of narcissists and their manipulation tactics is a crucial step in protecting yourself from toxic relationships. Whether you are dealing with an overt, covert, malignant, somatic, or cerebral narcissist, understanding their behavior allows you to set boundaries and take back control of your life. The more you learn about these tactics, the better equipped you will be to break free from unhealthy dynamics and heal from past emotional wounds.

Chapter 5:
The Cycle of Narcissistic Abuse

Narcissistic abuse follows a predictable and deeply damaging pattern that traps victims in emotional and psychological turmoil. This cycle—consisting of idealization, devaluation, and discard—ensnares victims by making them doubt their reality, self-worth, and ability to leave the relationship. Understanding this cycle is crucial for recognizing narcissistic abuse, breaking free from it, and ultimately healing.

The Stages: Idealization, Devaluation, and Discard

A relationship with a narcissist does not start with obvious abuse. Instead, narcissists lure their victims in with charm, attention, and love before systematically breaking them down. This cycle can repeat multiple times, reinforcing trauma bonds that make it incredibly difficult for victims to escape.

Stage One: Idealization – The Trap of Perfection

In the idealization phase, the narcissist appears to be everything the victim ever wanted. This phase is often referred to as "love bombing" in romantic relationships, but it applies to friendships, family dynamics, and workplace relationships as well.

During this phase, the narcissist:

- Showers the victim with excessive attention, flattery, and affection.
- Mirrors the victim's values, interests, and desires, making them feel deeply understood.
- Places the victim on a pedestal, making them feel special and unique.
- Moves quickly in the relationship, often talking about a future together early on.

This stage is intoxicating. The victim feels euphoric, believing they have found an extraordinary connection. However, this is not genuine love or admiration—it is a calculated strategy to gain trust and control.

The idealization phase is so powerful that when the narcissist later becomes cruel or indifferent, the victim often clings to memories of how things "used to be," believing that if they try hard enough, they can bring back that perfect version of the narcissist.

Stage Two: Devaluation – The Emotional Rollercoaster

Once the victim is emotionally invested, the narcissist's behavior shifts. The same person who once adored and praised them now criticizes, belittles, and manipulates them. This transition is often slow and subtle, making it difficult for the victim to recognize what is happening.

Signs of the devaluation phase include:

- Criticism and belittling: The narcissist makes hurtful remarks, insults, or sarcastic comments disguised as "jokes."
- Gaslighting: They deny past promises or events, making the victim question their memory and perception.
- Silent treatment: They withdraw affection and communication to punish the victim.
- Triangulation: They compare the victim to others, making them feel inadequate and desperate for approval.
- Emotional unpredictability: They alternate between affection and cruelty, keeping the victim in a constant state of anxiety.

During devaluation, the narcissist slowly erodes the victim's self-worth, making them feel unlovable, inadequate, or even crazy. The victim desperately tries to regain the narcissist's approval, blaming themselves for the shift in behavior and working harder to "fix" the relationship.

Stage Three: Discard – The Cold and Sudden Exit

The discard phase is one of the most painful aspects of narcissistic abuse. After breaking the victim down emotionally, the narcissist abruptly ends the relationship—often without warning or explanation. The victim is left feeling worthless, abandoned, and confused.

Common discard behaviors include:

- Sudden abandonment: The narcissist disappears without closure, leaving the victim blindsided.
- Replacing the victim quickly: Often, the narcissist has already lined up a new target and moves on immediately.
- Blaming the victim: They rewrite history, painting themselves as the victim and the actual victim as the problem.
- Public humiliation: Some narcissists smear the victim's reputation, spreading lies to mutual friends or colleagues.

The discard phase is especially painful because, after the intense idealization stage, the victim is left feeling empty and discarded, as if they never truly mattered. The emotional contrast is devastating.

However, the cycle doesn't always end here. Many narcissists hoover—a manipulation tactic where they try to re-enter the victim's life with false promises of change. If the victim falls for this, the cycle starts over, leading to more abuse.

How the Cycle Perpetuates Itself

Narcissistic abuse does not happen in isolation—it is reinforced by deep psychological and emotional factors that make it difficult for victims to leave.

Trauma Bonding: The Psychological Chains

One of the main reasons victims struggle to escape narcissistic abuse is trauma bonding—a psychological phenomenon where the victim forms a powerful emotional attachment to their abuser. This occurs because of the intermittent reinforcement of love and cruelty.

- When the narcissist is kind, the victim feels relief and hope.
- When the narcissist is cruel, the victim tries harder to regain their love.

Over time, the brain becomes addicted to these emotional highs and lows, making it extremely difficult for the victim to leave, even when they recognize the abuse.

Cognitive Dissonance: The Battle Between Reality and Fantasy

Cognitive dissonance occurs when a person holds conflicting beliefs. In an abusive relationship, the victim struggles to reconcile the loving, charming side of the narcissist with their cruel, abusive side.

- The mind tries to rationalize the abuse.
- The victim focuses on past good moments, believing they can return.
- They blame themselves rather than seeing the narcissist's pattern.

This mental conflict keeps the victim trapped, believing that if they just behave differently, they can fix the relationship.

Fear and Emotional Dependence

- Victims often develop a deep fear of leaving due to:
- Emotional dependency: The narcissist has convinced them they are unlovable or incapable of being without them.
- Threats and intimidation: Narcissists may threaten the victim with financial ruin, social isolation, or even harm if they try to leave.
- Guilt and obligation: The victim may feel responsible for the narcissist's well-being, believing they must stay to help them.

These fears make it incredibly difficult to break free.

Societal and Family Pressure

Many victims stay because of external pressures:

- Cultural expectations: Some cultures or religious beliefs discourage leaving relationships, no matter how abusive they are.
- Family dynamics: Victims may have been raised in toxic environments where they learned to tolerate abuse.
- Financial dependence: Some narcissists control their victims financially, making escape seem impossible.

These factors create an overwhelming sense of helplessness, reinforcing the cycle of abuse.

Breaking the Cycle

Understanding the cycle of narcissistic abuse is the first step in breaking free. Recognizing that narcissists do not change—no matter how many times they promise—helps victims detach emotionally and rebuild their sense of self.

Steps to break the cycle include:

1. Educate Yourself: Learn about narcissistic abuse to recognize manipulation tactics.
2. Set Boundaries: Enforce firm limits to protect yourself from further harm.
3. Seek Support: Find a therapist or support group that understands narcissistic abuse.
4. Go No Contact or Use Grey Rock: If possible, cut off all communication with the narcissist. If you must interact (co-parenting, work, etc.), limit engagement to neutral, emotionless responses.
5. Rebuild Self-Worth: Focus on healing, self-care, and regaining confidence.

Breaking free from narcissistic abuse is not easy, but it is possible. With awareness, support, and inner strength, victims can reclaim their lives and never fall into the cycle again.

Part II: The Empath's Experience

This section shifts the focus from understanding narcissism to the lived experience of those who find themselves entangled with narcissists—particularly empaths. Empaths are deeply sensitive individuals with a heightened ability to feel and absorb the emotions of others. While this trait makes them compassionate and nurturing, it can also make them vulnerable to the manipulations of narcissists.

The relationship between an empath and a narcissist is often described as a toxic dance—one partner constantly taking while the other gives to the point of exhaustion. This section will explore why empaths are drawn to narcissists, the psychological and emotional toll of these relationships, and how to recognize red flags before it's too late.

Readers will gain insight into their own patterns, understand how their empathy is being weaponized against them, and start the journey toward reclaiming their power. Whether you are an empath who has suffered at the hands of a narcissist or someone who wants to understand this dynamic better, this section will provide the tools to recognize, process, and heal from the effects of narcissistic abuse.

Now, let's explore the empath's profile, their vulnerabilities, and how narcissists exploit their kindness.

Chapter 6:

The Empath's Profile

Key Traits and Characteristics

Empaths are individuals with an extraordinary ability to tune into the emotions, energy, and needs of those around them. Unlike most people, who may sympathize with others to a certain extent, empaths physically and emotionally absorb the feelings of others as if they were their own. This heightened sense of perception can be both a blessing and a curse, shaping their experiences, relationships, and even their mental health. Understanding the key traits and characteristics of an empath can provide insight into why they are so deeply affected by relationships with narcissists and why they often struggle to break free from these toxic dynamics.

Extreme Emotional Sensitivity

Empaths are highly sensitive to the emotions of others. Whether it's joy, sadness, anger, or fear, they pick up on emotional energy in their environment almost instinctively. This sensitivity extends beyond just the spoken word; empaths notice micro-expressions, body language, and the slightest shift in tone or energy. While this trait allows them to connect with others on a deep level, it can also become overwhelming, particularly in high-stress environments or when surrounded by negativity.

For example, an empath might walk into a room and immediately sense tension before anyone says a word. They can feel the underlying emotions in a conversation, even when people are trying to hide their true feelings. This level of awareness makes them excellent at comforting others, offering support, and intuitively knowing what someone needs. However, it also makes them highly susceptible to emotional exhaustion, especially when dealing with manipulative individuals like narcissists who use emotions as a weapon.

Deep Compassion and Desire to Heal Others

One of the most defining traits of an empath is their innate drive to help, heal, and support others. They feel an almost compulsive need to ease the suffering of those around them, often putting others' needs above their own. This selflessness is a beautiful quality, but it can also make them vulnerable to people who take advantage of their kindness.

Because empaths genuinely want to help others, they are particularly drawn to people who are broken, wounded, or emotionally unavailable—qualities often found in narcissists. Narcissists, despite their outward confidence and grandiosity, are deeply insecure individuals who often carry unresolved childhood wounds. Empaths sense this pain beneath the narcissist's facade and believe they can "fix" them with enough love, patience, and understanding. Unfortunately, this mindset often traps them in toxic relationships where they continue to give without receiving anything in return.

Absorbing the Emotions of Others

Empaths don't just understand what others are feeling; they feel it themselves. This ability, known as emotional absorption, can be overwhelming and draining. If a loved one is sad, an empath might find themselves feeling sad as well, even if nothing in their own life is wrong. This can lead to emotional burnout, particularly when they are in relationships with narcissists, who frequently create emotional chaos.

When involved with a narcissist, the empath is subjected to constant mood swings, manipulation, and emotional highs and lows. Because they absorb these emotions so deeply, it can feel like they are carrying the weight of the narcissist's dysfunction on their own shoulders. Over time, this can lead to chronic anxiety, depression, and self-doubt, as they begin to lose sight of where their own emotions end and the narcissist's emotions begin.

Highly Intuitive and Spiritually Connected

Empaths often have a strong sense of intuition, sometimes described as a "sixth sense" or gut feeling. They can sense dishonesty, hidden motives, and subtle shifts in energy before anyone else does. This intuition can serve as a powerful guide in their lives, helping them navigate relationships and make decisions that align with their well-being.

However, when in a relationship with a narcissist, this intuition is often dismissed, gaslighted, or ignored. Narcissists are skilled at making empaths doubt their own instincts, convincing them that their perceptions are wrong. Over time, the empath may lose trust in their own intuition, leading to confusion, self-doubt, and an inability to distinguish truth from manipulation.

Overwhelmed in Crowded or Intense Environments

Because empaths absorb so much emotional energy, they often find large crowds, conflict, or high-stress environments overwhelming. They may need more alone time than the average person to recharge and process their emotions. Unlike narcissists, who thrive on attention and external validation, empaths tend to feel drained after prolonged social interactions, especially if those interactions involve negative or aggressive energy.

This trait makes them more likely to isolate themselves, particularly when they are caught in a toxic relationship. The narcissist, recognizing this, often exacerbates their need for isolation by controlling their social interactions, making them feel guilty for wanting time alone, or subtly discouraging them from maintaining outside relationships.

Difficulty Setting Boundaries

Perhaps one of the most dangerous traits of an empath in a narcissistic relationship is their struggle with boundaries. Because they feel other people's pain so deeply, they often find it difficult to say no, even when something is hurting them. They fear that setting boundaries will disappoint or hurt others, leading them to overextend themselves emotionally, physically, and mentally.

Narcissists exploit this weakness by pushing past the empath's limits, demanding constant attention, and making them feel guilty for asserting their needs. The more the empath sacrifices, the more the narcissist takes, creating a cycle where the empath becomes drained and the narcissist continues to feed off their energy.

A Strong Sense of Justice and Fairness

Empaths have a deep-rooted desire for justice, fairness, and truth. They cannot stand to see others being mistreated and often go out of their way to defend those who are vulnerable. This makes them natural advocates, healers, and nurturers. However, this strong sense of justice can also make them a target for narcissists, who use deception, manipulation, and power plays to get what they want.

When a narcissist is confronted about their behavior, they rarely take accountability. Instead, they shift blame, play the victim, or turn the tables on the empath, making them feel like they are the problem. The empath, unable to comprehend such blatant dishonesty, often tries harder to "prove" their good intentions, further entrenching themselves in the narcissist's web of control.

Empaths possess a unique set of traits that allow them to connect deeply with others, offer genuine compassion, and navigate the world with heightened intuition. However, these same traits also make them vulnerable to toxic relationships—especially with narcissists. Their desire to help, their emotional sensitivity, and their difficulty setting boundaries create the perfect storm for emotional manipulation and abuse.

Understanding these traits is the first step toward empowerment. By recognizing their own tendencies, empaths can begin to set healthier boundaries, protect their energy, and make choices that prioritize their well-being. While their ability to love deeply is a gift, it should never come at the cost of their own mental and emotional health.

Strengths and Vulnerabilities in Relationships

Empaths experience relationships in a profoundly deep and meaningful way. They bring intense emotional awareness, compassion, and understanding to their connections with others, making them exceptional partners, friends, and caregivers. However, these very qualities can also make them vulnerable, particularly in toxic relationships with manipulative individuals like narcissists.

Understanding both the strengths and vulnerabilities of an empath in relationships is essential for personal growth, boundary-setting, and fostering healthier connections. Let's explore these aspects in depth.

The Strengths of an Empath in Relationships

1. Deep Emotional Connection

One of the most remarkable strengths of an empath is their ability to form deep emotional bonds. Unlike individuals who struggle with emotional intimacy, empaths naturally connect with others on a soul level. They don't just listen; they truly hear and feel the emotions of their loved ones.

This makes them incredibly supportive partners who can offer a safe space for emotional expression. Their ability to understand unspoken feelings helps their loved ones feel valued, heard, and emotionally secure. People are naturally drawn to empaths because of this nurturing energy, as it creates a profound sense of belonging and acceptance.

However, this strength can also be a double-edged sword. When paired with the wrong partner—someone emotionally unavailable, manipulative, or abusive—the empath may feel the weight of the entire relationship on their shoulders. Their deep emotional connection can become a burden, especially if their partner is incapable of reciprocating in a meaningful way.

2. Natural Caregiving and Nurturing

Empaths are born caregivers. They instinctively offer comfort, support, and healing to those in distress. This nurturing nature makes them wonderful partners who go above and beyond to ensure their loved ones feel safe and cared for.

In healthy relationships, this can create a strong, loving dynamic where both partners support and uplift each other. However, in toxic relationships, this strength can quickly turn into self-sacrifice. Empaths often find themselves constantly giving while receiving little in return. Their willingness to "fix" or "heal" others can lead them into relationships with emotionally damaged or toxic individuals who take advantage of their kindness.

A narcissist, for example, may present themselves as a victim early in the relationship, drawing the empath in with a sob story. The empath, feeling a deep need to help, invests all their energy into "saving" this person. But narcissists don't want to be saved—they want control. Over time, the empath's nurturing nature is exploited, leaving them emotionally depleted.

3. Highly Intuitive and Perceptive

Empaths possess a heightened sense of intuition, allowing them to pick up on subtle emotional cues and unspoken truths. They can often sense when something is off in a relationship before any clear signs emerge.

This intuitive ability helps them navigate complex emotional dynamics and protect themselves from dishonest or harmful individuals. However, many empaths struggle to trust their intuition when dealing with a manipulative partner. Gaslighting—a common tactic used by narcissists—causes the empath to second-guess their instincts, leading them to ignore red flags they would otherwise recognize.

For instance, an empath might sense that their partner is lying about something, but when confronted, the narcissist may turn the tables, accusing the empath of being paranoid or overly sensitive. Over time, this repeated manipulation causes the empath to doubt their inner voice, making them more susceptible to further mistreatment.

4. Strong Sense of Loyalty and Commitment

Empaths are incredibly loyal and dedicated to their relationships. They believe in unconditional love and will go to great lengths to support their partner through difficult times. This level of commitment makes them reliable and trustworthy, fostering deep and meaningful connections.

However, this loyalty can sometimes blind them to toxic behaviors. An empath may stay in an abusive relationship far longer than they should because they believe in the potential for change. They see the good in people and often cling to the positive moments, hoping that love, patience, and understanding will eventually transform the relationship.

Unfortunately, this unwavering loyalty makes them prime targets for narcissists, who thrive on control and manipulation. The longer an empath stays, the more difficult it becomes to leave, as their deep emotional investment makes them feel responsible for the relationship's success or failure.

5. The Ability to Inspire and Heal Others

Because of their deep emotional insight and compassion, empaths often inspire and uplift those around them. They have a way of making people feel understood, validated, and loved, which can have a profound healing effect on their relationships.

In healthy partnerships, this ability fosters growth, emotional security, and mutual appreciation. However, in relationships with toxic individuals, the empath's healing energy is drained rather than reciprocated. They may become an emotional dumping ground for their partner's unresolved issues, leaving them exhausted and emotionally depleted.

The Vulnerabilities of an Empath in Relationships

1. Difficulty Setting Boundaries

Empaths struggle with boundaries because they don't want to disappoint or hurt others. Their natural inclination is to give, and they often feel guilty for saying no—even when something is negatively affecting them.

This makes them highly susceptible to being taken advantage of, especially by manipulative individuals who test their limits. A narcissist, for example, will repeatedly push past an empath's boundaries, making them feel guilty for asserting their needs. Over time, the empath may begin to feel trapped, unable to break free from the toxic cycle.

2. Overwhelming Emotional Absorption

Because empaths absorb the emotions of others so deeply, they often experience emotional burnout. When in a toxic relationship, they may feel completely consumed by their partner's emotions, leaving little room for their own needs and self-care.

This can lead to chronic stress, anxiety, depression, and even physical symptoms like fatigue, headaches, and digestive issues. The empath's nervous system is constantly overstimulated, making it difficult to find peace and emotional stability.

3. Attracting Emotionally Unavailable Partners

Empaths tend to attract partners who are emotionally wounded, unavailable, or manipulative. They are drawn to "fixer-upper" relationships, believing that their love and support can heal their partner's emotional wounds.

This pattern often leads them into relationships with narcissists, sociopaths, or individuals who lack the capacity for deep emotional connection. The empath pours their energy into the relationship, only to be met with emotional neglect, manipulation, or abuse.

4. Struggling to Walk Away from Toxic Relationships

Because of their deep emotional investment and loyalty, empaths find it incredibly difficult to leave toxic relationships. They often hold onto hope that their partner will change, even in the face of consistent mistreatment.

They may rationalize their partner's behavior, blame themselves, or believe that if they just love harder, things will improve. This makes them susceptible to repeated cycles of abuse, as they struggle to break free from the emotional hold the toxic partner has over them.

Empaths bring extraordinary emotional depth, love, and healing into their relationships. Their ability to connect, nurture, and inspire makes them incredible partners when matched with someone who respects and reciprocates their energy.

However, these same qualities can become vulnerabilities when they are paired with manipulative individuals. By recognizing their strengths and learning to protect their energy, empaths can cultivate healthier relationships that honor their emotional well-being.

Understanding the balance between giving and receiving, trusting their intuition, and setting firm boundaries will allow empaths to experience love in a way that is fulfilling rather than depleting. Healing begins when they realize that their worth is not tied to how much they can fix others— but to how well they love and protect themselves.

Chapter 7:
The Toxic Dance: Empath and Narcissist Dynamics

The Initial Connection and "Love Bombing"

The first stage of an empath and narcissist's relationship is often intoxicating, intense, and almost too good to be true. It feels like fate, like the missing piece of a puzzle has finally clicked into place. The connection is immediate, overwhelming, and all-consuming. But beneath the surface, what appears to be a deep and powerful bond is actually a carefully orchestrated illusion designed to pull the empath into the narcissist's web. This phase is known as love bombing, and it is one of the most deceptive and dangerous tactics a narcissist employs.

The Allure of Instant Connection

When an empath meets a narcissist, it can feel like magic. From the very first interaction, the narcissist makes them feel uniquely understood, cherished, and desired. Unlike other relationships that develop gradually, this one accelerates at an unnatural pace. The narcissist showers their target with affection, attention, and admiration, making them believe they've finally found someone who truly sees and values them.

This phase is so intoxicating because it preys on the deep-seated needs of the empath—their longing for connection, their desire to be appreciated, and their innate wish to heal and nurture others. The narcissist carefully studies their target, mirroring their dreams, passions, and values to create an illusion of compatibility. They say all the right things, make grand romantic gestures, and seem to be everything the empath has ever wanted in a partner.

What makes love bombing so powerful is that it floods the brain with feel-good chemicals like dopamine and oxytocin. These hormones create an emotional high, reinforcing the belief that this connection is special and irreplaceable. Empaths, who naturally feel emotions more deeply, become particularly susceptible to this chemical reinforcement, making it even harder for them to recognize the manipulation at play.

Tactics Used in Love Bombing

Narcissists employ a variety of strategies during the love bombing phase, each designed to intensify the bond and gain emotional control over the empath. Some of the most common tactics include:

1. Excessive Compliments and Flattery

The narcissist showers their target with over-the-top praise from the very beginning. They tell the empath they are unlike anyone they've ever met. They admire their intelligence, beauty, kindness, and uniqueness. They use phrases like:

- "I've never felt this way about anyone before."
- "You're my soulmate. We were meant to find each other."
- "I can't believe someone as amazing as you exists."

While compliments are normal in healthy relationships, narcissists use them excessively to create an illusion of destiny and unparalleled connection. This builds an emotional dependency, making the empath feel special and deeply valued.

2. Constant Communication and Attention

In the beginning, narcissists make themselves omnipresent in their target's life. They send texts all day, call multiple times, and make plans constantly. If the empath doesn't respond immediately, the narcissist might act hurt or insecure, making them feel guilty for not reciprocating at the same intensity.

This bombardment of attention makes the empath feel important and wanted, but it also subtly erodes their independence. Without realizing it, they start prioritizing the narcissist over other relationships and personal interests.

3. Grand Romantic Gestures

Narcissists use extravagant displays of affection to overwhelm their target emotionally. This can include:

- Expensive gifts
- Surprise trips
- Dramatic public declarations of love
- Rapid talk of marriage or moving in together

These grand acts serve a dual purpose—they heighten emotional intensity while making it harder for the empath to leave later. The more invested they feel, the more difficult it becomes to walk away when things take a turn.

4. Mirroring and False Compatibility

Perhaps one of the most manipulative tactics in love bombing is mirroring—where the narcissist reflects the empath's values, interests, and dreams to create the illusion of a perfect match.

- If the empath loves a certain kind of music, the narcissist suddenly does too.
- If the empath dreams of traveling, the narcissist expresses the exact same desire.
- If the empath has deep spiritual beliefs, the narcissist claims to share them.

This mirroring technique makes the empath feel profoundly understood, reinforcing the illusion that they've found their true partner.

5. Creating a Fairytale Narrative

Narcissists often craft a dramatic love story, making the empath feel like they've stepped into a romance novel. They might claim that they have never loved anyone this deeply before or that they have been waiting for someone just like them. This sense of destiny and urgency is a powerful tool, causing the empath to ignore red flags and move too fast in the relationship.

Why Love Bombing Works on Empaths

- Empaths are particularly vulnerable to love bombing because of their open hearts and deep emotional capacity. They:
- Crave meaningful connections and believe in the goodness of others.
- Have a strong desire to help and heal those who are wounded.
- Are naturally trusting, assuming that others have the same intentions they do.
- Feel emotions intensely, making the highs of love bombing even more addictive.

Because of these traits, empaths struggle to see the deception behind the intense affection. They mistake infatuation for deep love, believing that the narcissist's overwhelming passion is real.

The Dark Side of Love Bombing

- Once the empath is fully invested in the relationship, the mask begins to slip. The grand gestures and constant attention start to fade, replaced by small criticisms, mood swings, and emotional withdrawal.
- The once adoring partner becomes distant and cold.
- Compliments are replaced with passive-aggressive jabs.
- The empath begins to feel confused and anxious, wondering what they did wrong.

This is the beginning of the devaluation phase, where the narcissist starts to chip away at the empath's self-worth. What once felt like an unbreakable bond now feels unstable and painful, leaving the empath desperate to regain the affection they once had.

The contrast between love bombing and devaluation is what makes narcissistic abuse so insidious. The empath, still addicted to the intoxicating love they once received, chases after the validation that is now being withheld. This creates a powerful trauma bond that keeps them trapped in the cycle.

Breaking Free from Love Bombing

- Recognizing love bombing for what it is is the first step in breaking free. Some key warning signs include:
- The relationship moves too fast (talk of marriage or deep commitment within weeks).
- Extreme flattery and idealization that feels over the top.
- Constant texting and calling that makes you feel emotionally overwhelmed.
- Love that feels "too perfect"—as if the person is your mirror image.
- Grand promises that seem unrealistic.

If you suspect you are experiencing love bombing, it's important to slow down and assess the relationship critically. Healthy love develops over time, with mutual respect and space for individual growth. No real connection should feel like an emotional rollercoaster.

Love bombing is one of the most deceptive forms of manipulation, designed to create dependency and blind devotion. While it may feel exhilarating in the beginning, it is a manufactured illusion meant to pull the empath into a toxic cycle of control. By understanding how love bombing works, empaths can protect themselves from falling into its trap and recognize authentic love—love that is steady, respectful, and free of hidden agendas.

This is just the beginning of the toxic dance between the empath and the narcissist. Next, we will explore why empaths are drawn to fix and heal, further deepening the cycle of emotional entanglement.

Why Empaths Are Drawn to Fix and Heal

Empaths are naturally compassionate, deeply feeling individuals who have an innate drive to help others. They feel the emotions of those around them as if they were their own, making them particularly sensitive to the pain, struggles, and unspoken wounds of others. This powerful emotional atonement creates a strong urge to heal, support, and uplift those who are suffering.

When an empath encounters a narcissist—someone who often carries deep emotional wounds, unresolved childhood trauma, and an unfulfilled need for validation—the empath is drawn in by an overwhelming need to fix them. They see the narcissist not as they are, but as a wounded soul in need of love and understanding. This desire to help and heal is precisely what traps the empath in the toxic dance with a narcissist.

The Caregiver Mentality of an Empath

One of the core traits of an empath is their caretaker mentality. From an early age, many empaths feel a strong responsibility to support and nurture others, often placing the needs of those around them before their own. They are naturally:

- Highly sensitive to emotional distress in others.
- Quick to offer support and reassurance, even at their own expense.
- Deeply moved by suffering, feeling a personal obligation to ease others' pain.

Narcissists, despite their external confidence and grandiosity, often carry hidden insecurities, self-doubt, and deep emotional wounds. Their inability to regulate their self-worth causes them to constantly seek external validation—a role that an empath instinctively steps into.

To an empath, the narcissist appears as someone who needs love, care, and patience. They believe that if they love them enough, understand them deeply enough, or stay long enough, they can somehow bring out the "real" person hidden beneath the narcissistic mask. This belief is what keeps them invested, even when the relationship becomes damaging.

Empaths and the Illusion of "Unconditional Love"

Empaths often believe in unconditional love—the idea that love should persist despite difficulties, imperfections, and struggles. This belief is beautiful in healthy relationships, but in the context of a narcissistic relationship, it becomes dangerous.

A narcissist does not respond to love and care in the same way a healthy individual would. While a secure partner would appreciate an empath's kindness and reciprocate their love, a narcissist sees it as an opportunity for control. They exploit the empath's giving nature, taking and taking without ever giving back.

Empaths mistakenly believe that if they just love harder, the narcissist will change. But in reality, no amount of love can heal someone who refuses to confront their own wounds. Narcissists do not seek love—they seek supply. They need admiration, validation, and emotional labor, but they do not offer true intimacy in return.

The Savior Complex and Its Dangers

Many empaths struggle with what is known as the savior complex—the belief that they can "save" or "fix" a broken person. They may feel called to heal others, often at great personal cost. The savior complex is particularly dangerous in narcissistic relationships because:

- The empath becomes emotionally drained, pouring their energy into someone who does not reciprocate.
- The narcissist never truly changes, but continues to take advantage of the empath's efforts.
- The empath begins to believe that their self-worth is tied to the narcissist's well-being, making it even harder to walk away.

Narcissists encourage this dynamic by presenting themselves as victims. They share tragic stories from their past, detailing childhood neglect, betrayals, or previous heartbreaks. These stories may be real, exaggerated, or entirely fabricated, but they serve one purpose—to make the empath feel responsible for their healing.

Why Empaths Stay Even When It Hurts

Empaths often ignore red flags because they see beyond the narcissist's behaviors to the pain beneath. They rationalize mistreatment with thoughts like:

- "They're acting out because they've been hurt before."
- "If I just love them enough, they will trust me and change."
- "They push me away, but deep down, I know they love me."

This mindset keeps empaths trapped in a cycle of self-sacrifice, continually investing in a relationship that only drains them. They mistake the occasional moments of tenderness from the narcissist as signs of progress, when in reality, these are calculated acts of manipulation designed to keep them from leaving.

The tragic irony is that the more the empath gives, the more the narcissist takes. Instead of feeling appreciated, the empath begins to feel exhausted, unappreciated, and emotionally depleted.

Breaking the Cycle: Why an Empath Cannot Heal a Narcissist

It is crucial for empaths to recognize that they cannot heal a narcissist. Healing is a personal choice, and narcissists rarely seek genuine change. Some key truths an empath must accept are:

1. You cannot love someone into changing. Real change comes from self-awareness and effort, neither of which a narcissist is willing to commit to.
2. Your emotional well-being matters. A relationship should not be one-sided, draining, or emotionally exhausting.
3. Compassion must have boundaries. Loving someone does not mean tolerating abuse or manipulation.
4. Walking away is not failing. Choosing yourself over a toxic relationship is a form of strength, not weakness.

Empaths must learn to redirect their healing energy toward themselves instead of trying to fix someone who does not want to be fixed. True healing comes from self-care, personal growth, and choosing relationships that are mutual, respectful, and nourishing

The empath's deep compassion and willingness to heal others is one of their greatest strengths, but it becomes a weakness when paired with a narcissist. Understanding that not everyone can be saved is a painful but necessary lesson.

Real love does not demand self-sacrifice, exhaustion, or constant struggle. It is reciprocal, respectful, and nurturing. By recognizing the toxic patterns of narcissistic relationships, empaths can break free and learn to direct their love toward people who genuinely appreciate, respect, and reciprocate it.

The next section will explore how narcissists exploit empathic tendencies, deepening the cycle of control and emotional exhaustion.

How Narcissists Exploit Empathic Tendencies

Narcissists are masters of emotional manipulation, and one of their most potent tools is exploiting the kindness, patience, and compassion of empaths. Empaths naturally seek to understand, heal, and nurture others, which makes them prime targets for narcissistic abuse. A narcissist doesn't see an empath's love and care as something to be cherished but as a resource to be extracted—a constant supply of validation, attention, and emotional energy.

In this chapter, we will explore the psychological strategies narcissists use to manipulate empaths, how they turn an empath's greatest strengths into weaknesses, and why breaking free from this cycle is essential for self-preservation.

Empaths Are "Supply" to a Narcissist

To a narcissist, people are not seen as individuals with their own needs and emotions. Instead, they are sources of narcissistic supply—people who can provide adoration, validation, attention, and emotional labor.

Empaths, with their deep compassion and strong emotional intelligence, are the perfect targets. Unlike emotionally detached or self-centered individuals who might ignore a narcissist's needs, empaths actively give love, attention, and care. They listen, validate, support, and try to understand the narcissist on a deep level.

The narcissist thrives on this unconditional emotional energy, but instead of reciprocating, they take more and more—draining the empath to the point of exhaustion.

The Narcissist's Toolkit: How They Exploit Empaths

A narcissist uses a combination of psychological tactics, manipulation, and control techniques to keep the empath trapped in the relationship. Below are some of the most common strategies they use.

1. Love Bombing: Setting the Trap

At the start of the relationship, a narcissist bombards the empath with attention, admiration, and affection. They mirror the empath's deepest desires, making them feel understood and cherished.

They say things like:

- "You're the only one who truly understands me."
- "I've never met someone as kind and special as you."
- "We are soulmates."

This creates an emotional bond, making the empath feel that they've found someone who truly sees and appreciates them. What the empath doesn't realize is that this phase is a trap, designed to make them emotionally dependent.

2. Guilt-Tripping and Playing the Victim

Once the narcissist has established emotional control, they begin using guilt as a weapon.

Empaths have an overwhelming sense of responsibility for the well-being of others, and narcissists exploit this by constantly presenting themselves as the victim.

They say things like:
- "I act this way because of my past trauma. You should understand."
- "Everyone else has abandoned me. You're the only one who truly cares."
- "You're just like everyone else if you leave me."

This manipulates the empath into staying, making them feel that if they leave, they are abandoning someone who needs them.

3. Gaslighting: Making the Empath Doubt Reality

Gaslighting is one of the most damaging tactics narcissists use. It involves manipulating the empath into questioning their own reality.

They say things like:
- "I never said that. You're imagining things."
- "You're too sensitive. You always overreact."
- "That never happened. You're making it up."

Over time, the empath begins to doubt their own memory, perception, and emotions. They start relying on the narcissist for their sense of reality, which gives the narcissist even more control.

4. Emotional Draining and Energy Vampirism

Narcissists thrive on emotional reactions—whether it's love, admiration, or even anger and frustration. They provoke empaths just to get a response, feeding off their emotions.

Empaths, who naturally want to resolve conflicts and create harmony, keep engaging in emotional discussions with the narcissist, hoping to find a solution. But the narcissist never wants a solution—they just want to keep the empath emotionally invested and drained.

The result? The empath is left exhausted, anxious, and emotionally depleted, while the narcissist feels energized by the drama and control.

5. The Silent Treatment and Withdrawal of Affection

When an empath begins to set boundaries or express their own needs, the narcissist punishes them by withdrawing love and attention.

They suddenly become cold, distant, and unresponsive. This triggers an anxiety response in the empath, who panics and tries harder to fix the relationship.

The narcissist uses this fear of abandonment to keep the empath chasing after their approval, even when the relationship is one-sided and toxic.

6. Creating Dependency

Narcissists make sure their victims feel like they cannot survive without them.

They will:

- Isolate the empath from friends and family.
- Undermine their confidence with subtle criticisms.
- Destroy their self-esteem, making them feel worthless without the narcissist.

The empath, who once felt independent and strong, now feels lost and broken—completely dependent on the narcissist for validation and purpose.

Why Narcissists Target Empaths Specifically

Narcissists don't choose just anyone to manipulate—they specifically seek out empaths because of their unique qualities:

1. Empaths forgive easily – Even after being hurt, they try to understand the narcissist's behavior and give them another chance.
2. Empaths blame themselves – Instead of recognizing the narcissist's abuse, they believe they just need to "be better" to fix the relationship.
3. Empaths crave deep connections – They mistake trauma bonds for true love, believing the relationship is intense because of their special connection.

4. Empaths have a strong moral code – They cannot comprehend how someone could intentionally manipulate and hurt them, so they keep giving the narcissist the benefit of the doubt.

Because of these qualities, narcissists see empaths as an endless source of emotional energy—someone they can drain without consequences.

Breaking Free: How Empaths Can Protect Themselves

- To escape this cycle, empaths must recognize their own worth and set firm boundaries. Some key steps include:
- Understanding that love should be mutual – If a relationship constantly drains you, it's not love—it's exploitation.
- Trusting your instincts – If something feels wrong, don't ignore the red flags.
- Practicing emotional detachment – Not every wounded soul is your responsibility to heal.
- Setting clear boundaries – Learn to say NO without guilt.
- Cutting off toxic connections – The best way to heal is to remove yourself from the source of harm.

By reclaiming their power, empaths can break free from the toxic grip of a narcissist and build a life that is based on mutual love, respect, and emotional balance.

Empaths are naturally giving, compassionate, and loving individuals, but these very qualities make them vulnerable to narcissistic exploitation. The key to breaking free is recognizing that love should not come at the cost of your own well-being.

A narcissist will never change for an empath, no matter how much love, patience, and care is given. The only way forward is to prioritize self-respect, set boundaries, and choose relationships that bring true emotional fulfilment.

The next part will explore how to break the cycle and begin the healing process.

Chapter 8:

Emotional Impact and Recognizing the Red Flags

The emotional and psychological toll of a relationship with a narcissist can be devastating. Those who have experienced narcissistic abuse often find themselves struggling with anxiety, depression, PTSD, and a deep sense of self-doubt. The damage is not just emotional; it alters the way victims see themselves, their relationships, and the world. Recognizing the red flags of narcissistic behavior is crucial to breaking free and preventing further harm. This chapter explores the profound emotional impact of narcissistic abuse, provides a comprehensive checklist for identifying narcissistic patterns, and emphasizes the importance of trusting your intuition in detecting and avoiding toxic relationships.

Psychological and Emotional Toll: Anxiety, Depression, PTSD, and Low Self-Esteem

Narcissistic abuse is often insidious, slowly chipping away at the victim's self-worth and mental health. By the time someone realizes they have been in an abusive relationship, they may already be suffering from severe emotional and psychological distress. The effects can be long-lasting, affecting their ability to trust, form new relationships, and function in everyday life.

Anxiety: Walking on Eggshells

One of the most common consequences of narcissistic abuse is chronic anxiety. Victims often find themselves in a constant state of hyper-vigilance, never knowing what will set the narcissist off. They become conditioned to anticipate mood swings, manipulation, or punishment, leading to high levels of stress hormones like cortisol and adrenaline.

People in relationships with narcissists frequently develop obsessive overthinking patterns, replaying conversations in their minds, questioning whether they said or did something wrong. This anxiety can manifest physically, leading to symptoms such as:

- Rapid heartbeat and shortness of breath
- Insomnia and nightmares
- Digestive issues due to prolonged stress
- Chronic fatigue and headaches

Over time, this constant state of fear and unpredictability erodes mental and physical well-being, leaving the victim emotionally exhausted.

Depression: The Emotional Collapse

Depression is another common outcome of narcissistic abuse. After prolonged periods of manipulation, gaslighting, and emotional neglect, victims start to feel worthless, hopeless, and emotionally numb. The idealization phase during the beginning of the relationship creates a sharp contrast to the eventual devaluation and discard, making the emotional pain even more intense.

Victims often report:

- A deep sense of sadness and emptiness
- Loss of interest in activities they once enjoyed
- Social withdrawal and isolation
- Feelings of guilt and shame, believing they are the problem

Because narcissists excel at making their victims feel at fault for everything, the burden of self-blame can be overwhelming.

PTSD and Complex Trauma

Many survivors of narcissistic abuse develop symptoms of post-traumatic stress disorder (PTSD) or complex PTSD (C-PTSD). Unlike traditional PTSD, which often results from a single traumatic event, C-PTSD develops from prolonged emotional and psychological abuse.

Symptoms include:

- Flashbacks and intrusive memories of past arguments, gaslighting incidents, or traumatic events
- Emotional dysregulation, where the person feels sudden surges of anger, fear, or sadness without understanding why
- Avoidance behaviors, such as being unable to engage in certain conversations, fearing relationships, or avoiding reminders of the narcissist
- Hyper-vigilance, always being on edge, waiting for the next "attack"

C-PTSD is particularly damaging because it rewires the brain's ability to process stress, making it difficult for survivors to feel safe—even after the narcissist is gone.

Low Self-Esteem and Identity Erosion

Narcissists methodically dismantle their victims' self-worth through constant criticism, invalidation, and blame-shifting. Over time, the victim begins to doubt their abilities, decisions, and even their sense of reality.

Common symptoms include:

- Self-doubt and inability to make decisions without reassurance
- Negative self-talk, believing they are unworthy or not good enough
- Fear of rejection, making them overly accommodating in relationships
- Loss of personal identity, feeling as though they don't know who they are outside of the relationship

This loss of self is one of the most painful aspects of narcissistic abuse. However, with awareness and healing, survivors can rebuild their sense of identity and self-worth.

A Checklist for Identifying Narcissistic Patterns

One of the biggest challenges in escaping narcissistic abuse is recognizing it in the first place. Many people don't realize they are in a toxic relationship until they are deeply entangled. Below is a checklist to help identify narcissistic behaviors:

1. They Love-Bomb You
    - Over-the-top compliments and affection early in the relationship
    - Rushing intimacy, claiming you are their "soulmate" too soon
    - Making you feel like you are on a pedestal, only to knock you down later
2. They Are Highly Manipulative
    - Twisting your words and making you feel guilty
    - Playing the victim to avoid accountability
    - Making promises they never keep
3. They Engage in Gaslighting
    - Denying things they clearly said or did
    - Making you question your memory and perception of reality
    - Telling you that you're "too sensitive" or "crazy"
4. They Control and Isolate You
    - Discouraging you from seeing friends and family
    - Monitoring your phone, social media, or whereabouts
    - Making you feel guilty for wanting independence
5. They Blame You for Everything
    - Refusing to take responsibility for their actions
    - Turning every argument around to make you the problem
    - Saying things like, "You made me do this"
6. They Give You the Silent Treatment
    - Ignoring you for hours or days as punishment
    - Withholding affection or attention to control you
    - Making you feel invisible and worthless
7. They Discard You When You No Longer Serve Them
    - Suddenly losing interest in you for no apparent reason
    - Devaluing and replacing you with someone else
    - Acting as if you never mattered once they are done with you

If several of these behaviors feel familiar, you may be in a toxic or abusive relationship with a narcissist. Recognizing these red flags early on can help you protect yourself from deeper emotional damage.

Trusting Your Intuition

One of the most powerful tools a person has against narcissistic abuse is their own intuition. However, many victims of narcissists learn to ignore or distrust their gut feelings due to prolonged gaslighting.

Signs That Your Intuition Is Warning You

1. You Feel Uneasy Around the Narcissist – Even if nothing obvious is happening, your body tenses up when they enter the room.
2. You Constantly Justify Their Behavior – You find yourself making excuses for their cruelty or inconsistency.
3. Your Emotions Are Up and Down – You feel euphoric when they are kind but devastated when they are cold.
4. You Sense a Pattern of Deception – Even if you can't prove it, you feel like they are hiding something.
5. You Are Afraid of Speaking Up – You hesitate to express your needs or opinions because you fear their reaction.

Rebuilding Trust in Your Intuition

- Practice self-reflection through journaling and meditation.
- Listen to how your body reacts—if you feel drained or anxious after interacting with someone, that's a sign.
- Talk to trusted friends or therapists who can help validate your experiences.

Trusting your instincts is a vital part of healing. The more you honor your intuition, the stronger and more resilient you will become.

The emotional impact of narcissistic abuse is profound, leaving victims with anxiety, depression, PTSD, and shattered self-esteem. Recognizing the red flags of narcissistic behavior is crucial for avoiding further harm. By learning to trust your intuition, you can begin to break free from toxic cycles and move toward a life of self-empowerment and healing.

Part III: Breaking the Cycle and Healing

Escaping the grip of narcissistic abuse is not just about leaving the relationship—it's about reclaiming your identity, healing from emotional wounds, and building a future free from toxic patterns. Many survivors struggle with self-doubt, lingering trauma, and the fear of repeating past mistakes. This section focuses on empowering survivors with the tools they need to break the cycle, heal, and thrive.

Healing from narcissistic abuse requires setting boundaries, practicing self-care, seeking professional support, and rebuilding self-worth. Each chapter in this section will guide you through practical steps, psychological insights, and transformative strategies to help you regain control over your life.

Chapter 9:
Setting Boundaries and Establishing Detachment

Escaping the toxic grip of a narcissist is not just about physically leaving—it's about reclaiming your mind, emotions, and personal power. Setting boundaries is one of the most challenging yet empowering steps in this process. Narcissists thrive on control, and their manipulation is most effective when their victims lack clear boundaries. The moment you start setting firm limits, you disrupt their power over you.

For empaths, this can be difficult. Empaths are naturally compassionate, forgiving, and understanding—qualities that narcissists exploit and abuse. Many survivors struggle with guilt, self-doubt, and fear of retaliation when trying to enforce boundaries. However, boundaries are not about punishing the narcissist; they are about protecting yourself.

This chapter will guide you through the importance of boundaries, how to establish and enforce them, and the powerful techniques of No Contact and Grey Rock that allow you to break free from the cycle of narcissistic manipulation.

The Importance of Boundaries

What Are Boundaries and Why Do They Matter?

Boundaries are the guidelines we set to define how we allow ourselves to be treated. They determine what is acceptable and what is not. Healthy relationships—whether with friends, family, or romantic partners—are built on mutual respect for each other's boundaries.

But in relationships with narcissists, boundaries are ignored, violated, or manipulated. A narcissist will:

- Push past your comfort zone to test how much control they have.
- Guilt-trip or gaslight you into believing your boundaries are selfish or unreasonable.

- Exploit your empathy to make you feel responsible for their emotions.
- Punish you with silent treatment or rage when you try to enforce limits.

Narcissists view boundaries as threats to their control. They don't want you to have a sense of autonomy because that would mean they can no longer manipulate you.

Why Empaths Struggle with Setting Boundaries

Empaths are natural givers. They believe in second chances, understanding, and emotional connection. While these qualities make them wonderful, compassionate individuals, they also make them prime targets for narcissists.

If you've ever thought:

- "Maybe I'm overreacting."
- "I don't want to upset them."
- "If I just explain it better, they'll understand."
- "I feel guilty saying no."

Then you are struggling with boundary-setting. And that's okay. Learning to prioritize your own well-being is a skill that takes time—but it is essential for breaking free from toxic relationships.

Signs That You Need Stronger Boundaries

- If you recognize any of these patterns in your relationships, it's time to establish firmer boundaries:
- You feel emotionally drained after interacting with someone.
- You suppress your feelings to avoid conflict.
- You struggle to say "no" without guilt.
- You feel responsible for managing others' emotions.
- You experience anxiety or dread before seeing a certain person.

If this sounds familiar, don't blame yourself. Instead, recognize that you have the power to change it.

Practical Strategies for Boundary Setting

Step 1: Define Your Boundaries Clearly

The first step to enforcing boundaries is knowing exactly what they are. Many people in toxic relationships don't realize they have never been allowed to have boundaries.

Take time to ask yourself:

- What behaviors make me feel uncomfortable, disrespected, or unsafe?
- Where do I need more space, privacy, or emotional protection?
- What am I no longer willing to tolerate?
- Your boundaries will be unique to you, but here are some examples:
- Emotional Boundaries: "I will not allow anyone to minimize my feelings."
- Time Boundaries: "I will not overextend myself for others at the expense of my well-being."

Physical Boundaries: "I do not owe anyone access to my body or personal space."

Communication Boundaries: "I will not engage in conversations that are hostile, manipulative, or draining."

Step 2: Communicate Boundaries with Confidence

Narcissists thrive on vagueness and loopholes. If your boundaries are unclear, they will twist your words to keep their control.

Instead of saying:

"I don't like when you raise your voice."

Say:

"If you continue yelling at me, I will leave the conversation."

Instead of saying:

"I wish you wouldn't criticize me so much."

Say:

"If you continue to insult me, I will end this discussion."

Your boundaries should be firm, direct, and non-negotiable.

Step 3: Enforce Boundaries with Consequences

A narcissist will test you. If you set a boundary but don't follow through, they will see it as an empty threat and keep pushing.

Examples of enforcing consequences:

- If they insult you → End the conversation and walk away.
- If they ignore your requests → Refuse to engage.
- If they manipulate you → Block their number and limit contact.

Boundaries are not just about what you say—they are about what you DO.

When and How to Use No Contact or Grey Rock Techniques

No Contact: The Ultimate Boundary

The No Contact rule is the most powerful way to cut off a narcissist's control over you. It involves:

- Blocking their number, emails, and social media.
- Refusing to engage if they reach out through others.
- Avoiding places where you might run into them.

Benefits of No Contact:

Removes their ability to manipulate or guilt-trip you.

Gives you the space to heal.

Stops the cycle of abuse.

When No Contact Isn't an Option

If you must maintain contact (e.g., co-parenting or work), the Grey Rock Method is a powerful alternative.

The Grey Rock Technique: Becoming Uninteresting

The Grey Rock Method is a strategy where you become as dull and unresponsive as possible to a narcissist.

How to use Grey Rock:

- Keep responses short and unemotional (e.g., "Okay," "I don't know," "Sure").
- Avoid giving personal details or reacting emotionally.
- Speak in a neutral, monotone voice.
- Keep conversations strictly about necessary topics.

By depriving them of drama, emotion, or attention, they lose interest and seek their supply elsewhere.

Mistakes to Avoid When Using No Contact or Grey Rock

1. Breaking No Contact Due to Guilt or Loneliness

Narcissists will fake remorse, promise change, or act like the victim to reel you back in. Stay strong.

2. Engaging in Arguments While Using Grey Rock

If you start defending yourself, they have won. Stay neutral.

3. Believing They Have Changed

True narcissists do not change without intense therapy—and even then, it is rare.

Concluding Thoughts on Setting Boundaries and Detachment

- Setting boundaries with a narcissist is not easy. They will resist, retaliate, and test your limits. But boundaries are not for them—they are for YOU.
- By establishing firm, unwavering limits, you take back control of your life. You show yourself that your needs matter, your voice matters, and your peace matters.
- You are no longer their emotional puppet. You are free.
- And that is the first step toward true healing.

Chapter 10:
Embracing Self-Care and Self-Compassion

Surviving a relationship with a narcissist leaves deep emotional wounds. The pain may not always be visible, but it lingers in self-doubt, anxiety, depression, and a shattered sense of self-worth. Many survivors feel like a shell of who they once were, struggling to recognize themselves after enduring relentless manipulation, emotional abuse, and betrayal. But healing is possible, and it begins with embracing self-care and self-compassion.

For too long, your focus has been on the narcissist—their needs, their emotions, their demands—while you neglected your own. Now, it's time to turn inward and prioritize yourself. But self-care isn't just about bubble baths or spa days; it's about rebuilding your sense of self, reclaiming your emotional stability, and learning to treat yourself with the kindness you so freely gave to others.

This chapter will guide you through powerful healing practices, including mindfulness, meditation, and self-compassion—tools that will help you break free from the grip of narcissistic trauma and move toward inner peace, self-love, and emotional strength.

Mindfulness, Meditation, and Healing Practices

The Power of Mindfulness in Healing

Mindfulness is the practice of being fully present in the moment without judgment. For survivors of narcissistic abuse, this can be a challenge. You may find yourself trapped in the past, replaying painful memories, or anxious about the future, fearing that history will repeat itself. Mindfulness helps you shift your focus from the chaos of your thoughts to the present moment, allowing you to regain a sense of control and clarity.

One of the most insidious effects of narcissistic abuse is the erosion of self-trust. Narcissists manipulate reality, making you question your perceptions and instincts. Mindfulness helps you reconnect with yourself by:

- Teaching you to observe your emotions without being overwhelmed by them.
- Helping you recognize negative thought patterns and replace them with healthier ones.
- Allowing you to create emotional distance from painful memories and intrusive thoughts.

Mindfulness Techniques for Trauma Recovery

Practicing mindfulness doesn't require a major lifestyle change—it can be incorporated into your daily routine through simple exercises:

1. Grounding Techniques:

When anxiety strikes, bring yourself back to the present by focusing on your senses. Name:

- Five things you can see
- Four things you can touch
- Three things you can hear
- Two things you can smell
- One thing you can taste

This technique helps pull you out of rumination and emotional overwhelm.

2. Breathwork for Emotional Stability:

When triggered, take slow, deep breaths, inhaling for four seconds, holding for four seconds, and exhaling for four seconds.

This activates your parasympathetic nervous system, calming your body and mind.

3. Journaling with Awareness:

Set aside ten minutes daily to write freely about your thoughts and emotions.

Journaling allows you to process trauma, release emotions, and gain insight into recurring patterns.

The Role of Meditation in Healing

Meditation is a powerful tool for emotional regulation and self-awareness. When you've spent years being conditioned to focus on someone else's emotions, moods, and reactions, meditation teaches you to turn inward and reconnect with yourself.

Survivors of narcissistic abuse often experience hypervigilance—a constant state of anxiety, always anticipating the next attack. Meditation helps:

- Lower stress levels and reduce anxiety.
- Rewire your brain for emotional resilience.
- Develop inner peace, regardless of external chaos.

Meditation Practices for Survivors

1. Self-Compassion Meditation:

Find a quiet place and close your eyes.

Place your hand over your heart and repeat:

"I am worthy of love. I deserve kindness. I am healing, one breath at a time."

This reinforces self-love and emotional safety.

2. Guided Visualization:
   - Imagine yourself standing at the edge of a river.
   - Picture painful memories as leaves floating downstream.
   - Let them drift away, knowing you are no longer controlled by the past.
3. Loving-Kindness Meditation:

Repeat these phrases:

"May I be happy. May I be free. May I be at peace."

Then, extend this compassion to yourself, loved ones, and even those who hurt you—not for their sake, but to release yourself from resentment.

Cultivating Self-Compassion and Forgiveness

Why Self-Compassion Is Essential for Healing

After enduring narcissistic abuse, many survivors experience shame, self-blame, and self-criticism. You might think:

- "How did I let this happen?"
- "Why wasn't I strong enough to leave sooner?"
- "Maybe it really was my fault."

These thoughts are not the truth—they are the lingering effects of manipulation. Narcissists are experts at making their victims feel unworthy, inadequate, and at fault for everything. But healing requires learning to treat yourself with the same kindness and understanding you give others.

How to Practice Self-Compassion

1. Challenge Your Inner Critic:

Every time you catch yourself thinking, "I was so stupid for falling for them", replace it with:

- "I did the best I could with the knowledge I had."
- "I am learning and growing from this experience."
-

2. Reframe Your Story:

Instead of seeing yourself as a victim, recognize that you are a survivor who is reclaiming their power.

3. Treat Yourself Like a Friend:
- Imagine your best friend went through what you did.
- What would you say to them? Now, say that to yourself.

The Journey to Forgiveness

Forgiveness is one of the most misunderstood aspects of healing. Many people believe that forgiving a narcissist means excusing their behavior, allowing them back into your life, or pretending the abuse never happened. None of that is true.

Forgiveness is not about the narcissist—it is about freeing yourself from the emotional weight of resentment, anger, and pain. Holding onto rage keeps you tied to them; letting go breaks that bond and allows you to move forward.

How to Approach Forgiveness (Without Rushing the Process)

1. Acknowledge Your Pain:

Allow yourself to feel anger, sadness, and betrayal. These emotions are valid.

2. Redefine Forgiveness:

Forgiveness doesn't mean saying what they did was okay—it means saying you will no longer allow it to control you.

3. Forgive Yourself First:

The hardest part of healing is forgiving yourself for not leaving sooner, for ignoring red flags, or for believing their lies.

You didn't fail—you survived. And that is something to be proud of.

Conclusion Thoughts on Embracing Self-Care and Self-Compassion

Healing from narcissistic abuse is not a straight path—it's a journey with ups and downs, setbacks and breakthroughs. Some days, you will feel strong and free. Other days, the pain will resurface, and that's okay. Healing is not about perfection—it's about progress.

By embracing mindfulness, meditation, and self-compassion, you will slowly rebuild the person the narcissist tried to break. You are not what they said you were. You are strong. You are worthy. You are enough.

Keep going. Your healing is just beginning.

Chapter 11:
Seeking Therapy and Building Support

Surviving a relationship with a narcissist can leave deep, invisible wounds that linger long after the relationship has ended. The emotional abuse, manipulation, and gaslighting can leave you feeling confused, broken, and uncertain of your own reality. It's common to experience symptoms of anxiety, depression, post-traumatic stress disorder (PTSD), and self-doubt. You may have spent months or even years being conditioned to believe that your thoughts, feelings, and needs were invalid or unimportant.

But now, as you step forward on your journey to healing, you do not have to navigate this path alone. Therapy and support systems are powerful tools that can help you understand, process, and rebuild from the trauma of narcissistic abuse. Finding the right therapist, connecting with support groups, and accessing additional resources can be the difference between remaining trapped in the pain of the past and truly breaking free to reclaim your life.

This chapter will guide you through the process of finding a therapist who specializes in narcissistic abuse, exploring the benefits of support groups, and utilizing valuable resources that can aid in your healing journey.

Finding a Therapist Specialized in Narcissistic Abuse

Why Therapy Is Essential for Healing

After enduring a toxic relationship with a narcissist, it's natural to feel lost, overwhelmed, and unsure of how to move forward. Therapy provides a safe space to process your experiences, validate your emotions, and gain insight into how the abuse affected you.

A skilled therapist can help you:

- Recognize and validate the abuse you experienced, even if the narcissist convinced you it was "all in your head."
- Untangle the mental and emotional conditioning that made you doubt yourself.
- Learn strategies for setting healthy boundaries and protecting yourself from future toxic relationships.
- Rebuild self-esteem and confidence, which may have been shattered by years of manipulation.
- Develop coping mechanisms to manage PTSD, anxiety, and emotional triggers.
-

Choosing the Right Therapist

Not all therapists understand the complexities of narcissistic abuse. Some may downplay the effects, misunderstand the dynamics, or even push for reconciliation when cutting ties is the healthiest option. That's why it's crucial to find a therapist who:

1. Specializes in narcissistic abuse or trauma recovery – They should have experience working with survivors of emotional and psychological abuse.
2. Validates your experience – A good therapist will never question or minimize your pain. They will help you process your trauma with compassion and understanding.
3. Understands manipulation tactics – They should be well-versed in gaslighting, trauma bonding, love bombing, and emotional coercion.
4. Supports boundaries and healing – They won't encourage forgiveness or reconciliation if it compromises your well-being.
5. Uses trauma-informed approaches – Therapy should be a safe, empowering experience, not one that retraumatizes you.

Where to Find a Specialized Therapist

Finding a therapist who truly understands narcissistic abuse and emotional trauma can take time, but resources are available:

Online Directories:

- Psychology Today (www.psychologytoday.com) allows you to filter therapists by specialty.
- TherapyDen (www.therapyden.com) has trauma-informed therapists.
- Survivor Communities and Support Groups: Many survivors share recommendations for trauma-informed therapists.
- Local Domestic Abuse Shelters and Organizations: These groups often have referrals for therapists experienced in abuse recovery.
- Virtual Therapy Platforms: Websites like BetterHelp or Talkspace connect you with licensed professionals experienced in narcissistic abuse.

What to Expect in Therapy

Starting therapy can feel intimidating, especially if you were conditioned to suppress your emotions. But therapy is about you—your healing, your growth, your recovery.

In the first few sessions, your therapist will likely:

- Ask about your experiences to understand the nature of the abuse.
- Discuss your emotional and psychological symptoms (anxiety, depression, trauma responses).
- Work on rebuilding self-trust and confidence.
- Help you recognize and challenge negative thought patterns that were ingrained by the narcissist.
- Teach you coping strategies for dealing with triggers and emotional flashbacks.

Therapy isn't a quick fix—it's a journey of self-discovery and healing. Some days, it will feel like you're making incredible progress; other days, old wounds may resurface. Be patient with yourself. Healing takes time, but every session is a step toward freedom from the narcissist's control.

Utilizing Support Groups and Additional Resources

The Power of Community: Why Support Groups Matter

Narcissistic abuse can feel incredibly isolating. Many survivors feel alone in their experiences, questioning whether anyone truly understands what they've been through. A narcissist's manipulation often extends to friends and family, making it even harder to find validation and support.

This is where support groups become invaluable. Being in a space where others understand, validate, and share similar experiences can be incredibly healing.

Benefits of joining a support group:

- Validation: Hearing others' stories helps you realize you are not crazy, and you are not alone.
- Education: Many groups provide insights into narcissistic abuse, manipulation tactics, and recovery strategies.
- Emotional Support: Other survivors understand your pain in ways that even well-meaning loved ones may not.
- Encouragement and Hope: Seeing others heal gives you strength and motivation to keep going.

Where to Find Support Groups

1. Online Communities

Facebook groups like Narcissistic Abuse Survivors offer forums for discussion and support.

Reddit's r/NarcissisticAbuse is a space where survivors share stories, advice, and encouragement.

2. Local Support Groups

Many domestic violence shelters host abuse recovery meetings.

Meetup.com often has narcissistic abuse support groups in major cities.

3. Therapist-Led Groups

Some therapists run trauma recovery support groups for survivors.

These offer a structured healing environment with professional guidance.

4. Books and Podcasts

Books like The Body Keeps the Score (Bessel van der Kolk) and Healing from Hidden Abuse (Shannon Thomas) offer deep insights into trauma recovery.

Podcasts like The Narcissist Apocalypse share real survivor stories and expert advice.

Practical Steps for Building a Support System

1. Surround Yourself with Safe People

Identify friends or family who are supportive, nonjudgmental, and trustworthy.

If loved ones don't understand your experience, educate them with articles, books, or videos on narcissistic abuse.

2. Set Boundaries with Unsupportive Individuals

Some people may minimize your trauma or urge you to "just move on."

Protect your healing by limiting contact with those who invalidate your experiences.

3. Engage in Healing Activities

Join trauma-sensitive yoga classes to reconnect with your body.

Take up creative outlets (writing, painting, music) to express your emotions safely.

Spend time in nature, as it has profound healing benefits.

4. Be Patient with Yourself

Recovery isn't linear. Some days will feel strong, others overwhelming.

Progress happens in small steps—acknowledge each one.

Concluding Thoughts on Seeking Therapy and Building Support

Healing from narcissistic abuse isn't just about leaving the toxic relationship—it's about reclaiming your identity, your self-worth, and your inner peace. Therapy, support groups, and additional resources provide the tools you need to break free from emotional scars and rebuild a fulfilling life.

You do not have to heal alone. There is hope. There is support. And most importantly, there is a future beyond the pain.

You deserve healing. You deserve love. You deserve a life free from the shadows of narcissistic abuse. And that journey starts today.

Chapter 12:
Rebuilding Self-Worth and Moving Forward

Escaping the grasp of a narcissist is only the first step in the healing journey. The real challenge begins when you stand in front of the mirror and ask yourself: Who am I now? Years of manipulation, gaslighting, and emotional abuse can leave you feeling like a shell of who you once were, disconnected from your passions, your sense of self, and even your ability to trust others.

Rebuilding self-worth isn't just about healing—it's about rediscovering who you are, embracing your strengths, and stepping into a life that is truly yours. This chapter is dedicated to guiding you through that process.

We will explore:

- Rediscovering your identity and passions after years of suppression.
- Building and maintaining healthy relationships that nurture and uplift you.
- Practical strategies to ensure you never fall back into the cycle of narcissistic abuse.

This is your time to reclaim yourself.

Rediscovering Identity and Passions

The Loss of Self in Narcissistic Relationships

Narcissistic abuse often erodes your identity. Your likes, dislikes, dreams, and desires were constantly overshadowed by the narcissist's needs. You may have been made to feel that your passions were silly, your ambitions unrealistic, and your emotions inconvenient. Over time, you adapted—shifting, shrinking, and suppressing parts of yourself just to keep the peace.

Now that you're free, you may find yourself asking: Who am I, really?

This can feel overwhelming, but remember—your true self is still there, waiting to be rediscovered.

Steps to Reconnect with Yourself

1. Reflect on Who You Were Before the Narcissist

Think back to a time before the relationship. What did you love to do? What made you feel alive?

Did you enjoy reading? Painting? Traveling? Learning new things? Write these down and explore them again.

2. Try New Experiences

Healing is a journey of self-discovery. Give yourself permission to try things you've never done before. Take a dance class, travel alone, or start a new hobby.

The goal is not perfection but exploration—relearning how to find joy in life.

3. Reconnect with Your Inner Voice

When you were with the narcissist, your thoughts were often filtered through their expectations.

Start journaling or practicing mindfulness to hear your own voice again.

4. Set Small, Achievable Goals

Rebuilding self-worth requires action. Start with small, manageable goals that reinforce your sense of accomplishment.

Example: If you used to love painting, commit to creating one piece a week, even if it's just for yourself.

5. Surround Yourself with People Who See the Real You

Being around supportive, kind people will help you rediscover and embrace your authentic self.

Avoid people who pressure you to return to your old life or dismiss your healing process.

Rebuilding your identity isn't about going back to who you were—it's about becoming the strongest, most authentic version of yourself.

Forming Healthy Relationships

Breaking the Cycle of Toxic Relationships

One of the hardest parts of healing is realizing that, after enduring a narcissistic relationship, your perception of love and connection may be distorted. It's not your fault—narcissistic abuse conditions you to accept manipulation, inconsistency, and emotional unavailability as normal.

The good news? You can unlearn these patterns and build healthy, fulfilling relationships.

What a Healthy Relationship Looks Like

1. Mutual Respect – Your thoughts, feelings, and boundaries are honored.
2. Emotional Safety – You feel comfortable expressing yourself without fear of judgment or retaliation.
3. Consistent Support – Love isn't conditional or unpredictable.
4. Healthy Communication – Differences are discussed with understanding, not manipulation.
5. Independence – A healthy partner won't demand total control of your time and energy.

Steps to Rebuilding Trust in Relationships

1. Heal Before You Enter a New Relationship

Jumping into another relationship without healing can lead to repeating old patterns.

Take time to understand your needs, boundaries, and dealbreakers before opening up to someone new.

2. Set and Enforce Boundaries

Practice saying no without guilt.

Surround yourself with people who respect your limits, rather than testing them.

3. Pay Attention to Red Flags

If something feels off, trust your gut.

Watch for signs of love bombing, gaslighting, or boundary violations early on.

4. Learn to Accept Healthy Love

If you're used to chaotic love, stability may feel unfamiliar at first.

Remind yourself: Peace is not boring. Respect is not weakness. Real love is consistent and kind.

Not everyone deserves a place in your life. Choose relationships that support, uplift, and empower you.

Tips for a Future Free from Narcissistic Cycles

Healing is not just about escaping a toxic relationship—it's about ensuring you never fall into that cycle again. Here's how you can safeguard your future:

1. Know Your Worth

Your value is not determined by another person's approval.

Write down five qualities you love about yourself and remind yourself of them daily.

2. Trust Yourself Again

Narcissistic abuse makes you doubt your instincts. Rebuild trust in yourself by making small decisions daily and owning them.

Example: If something feels wrong in a conversation, acknowledge it instead of dismissing it.

3. Prioritize Self-Care

Emotional self-care: Journaling, therapy, meditation.

Physical self-care: Regular exercise, eating well, prioritizing sleep.

Social self-care: Spending time with uplifting, supportive people.

4. Keep Learning About Narcissistic Abuse

The more you understand how narcissists operate, the easier it is to spot and avoid them.

Read books, listen to survivor podcasts, and stay informed.

5. Take Things Slow in Future Relationships

Love bombing can feel like a fairytale, but it's often a red flag.

A healthy relationship builds slowly, based on mutual trust and respect.

6. Create a Life You Love—With or Without a Partner

You don't need a relationship to be whole. Focus on building a fulfilling, independent life where you feel happy on your own.

Pursue hobbies, career goals, and friendships that bring joy and purpose into your life.

Conclusion: Your Journey Forward

Escaping a narcissist's grasp was an act of courage. Healing from the damage they caused is an act of self-love. But the greatest victory? Rebuilding a life where you are free, thriving, and unapologetically yourself.

You are more than what happened to you. You are worthy of love, peace, and happiness.

As you move forward, remember:

You are not broken. You are healing.

You deserve respect, kindness, and love—from yourself and from others.

You are strong, resilient, and capable of creating a beautiful future.

This is your new beginning. Step into it with confidence, knowing that the best chapters of your life are still ahead of you.

Conclusion

Healing from narcissistic abuse is not just about surviving—it is about reclaiming yourself, your worth, and your life. If you have made it this far, if you have read and reflected on the truths laid out in this book, then know this: you are already on the path to healing.

Breaking free from the grip of a narcissist is one of the most courageous things a person can do. It requires you to go against everything they conditioned you to believe. It demands that you stand up for yourself, even when you feel like you have nothing left to give. It forces you to learn that the love you so freely gave to them was never meant to be thrown away—it was meant to be given back to yourself.

This book has not just been about understanding narcissism. It has been about you. About your pain, your resilience, your healing, and your future. It has been a journey through the dark corridors of emotional manipulation, psychological warfare, and deep wounds—but also a journey toward something far more powerful: hope, freedom, and self-reclamation.

You are not just someone who has been hurt. You are someone who has survived. And more than that—you are someone who is destined to thrive.

Recap of Key Takeaways

Let's take a moment to reflect on the most important lessons you've learned in this book. These are not just facts or theories; they are pieces of wisdom that will guide you for the rest of your life.

1. Understanding Narcissistic Personality Disorder (NPD)

Narcissism exists on a spectrum, from normal traits to full-blown NPD.

True narcissists lack empathy, crave power, and manipulate others for their own benefit.

Many narcissists were once victims themselves, but that does not excuse their actions.

2. Recognizing the Cycle of Narcissistic Abuse

The cycle follows Idealization, Devaluation, Discard, and Hoovering.

Love bombing is not real love—it is a tool of control.

The more you try to please a narcissist, the more they take from you.

3. The Empath's Experience

Empaths are deeply compassionate and drawn to helping others, which makes them prime targets for narcissists.

The narcissist thrives on your guilt, your forgiveness, and your willingness to see the good in them.

Healing starts when you realize you are not responsible for fixing them.

4. Breaking Free and Rebuilding Yourself

The only way to heal is through detachment—physically, mentally, and emotionally.

Boundaries are life-saving. They are not selfish. They are necessary.

No contact is one of the strongest acts of self-respect you will ever take.

Now, let's turn toward the most important part—what comes next.

Words of Hope and Encouragement

If you are reading this, I want you to pause. Take a deep breath. Feel the weight of everything you have been through, and then recognize this simple, undeniable truth:

You are still here.

That, in itself, is a victory.

For so long, you may have felt invisible. Unheard. Worthless. You may have looked in the mirror and not recognized the person staring back. You may have been gaslighted into doubting your own reality, made to believe that your emotions were "too much," your needs were "unreasonable," and your worth was defined by how useful you were to someone else.

But they were wrong.

You are not too much.

You are not unworthy.

You are not meant to live in the shadow of someone else's manipulation.

You were meant to shine. To love and be loved in return. To wake up and feel peace instead of anxiety. To live a life where your heart feels light instead of heavy.

You may not feel it yet. Healing is not linear. Some days, you will feel strong and free. Other days, you may find yourself longing for the narcissist's validation, even though you know they will never give it. That is normal. It does not mean you are weak—it means you are human.

The important thing is that you keep going. Even on the hardest days. Even when it feels impossible.

Because one day, without even realizing it, you will wake up and feel whole again.

And that day will be the beginning of the life you were always meant to live.

Concluding Thoughts on Breaking the Cycle of Narcissistic Abuse

Breaking free from a narcissist is not just about leaving them behind—it is about breaking the internal patterns that made you vulnerable to them in the first place.

Here are the most important steps in ensuring that you never fall back into the cycle again:

1. Trust Yourself Again

One of the most damaging things narcissistic abuse does is strip you of your self-trust. You may doubt your perceptions, your decisions, and even your own worth.

But your intuition was never wrong. The unease you felt? The red flags you noticed? They were real.

Trust yourself again. Your inner wisdom is powerful.

2. Boundaries Are Your Superpower

If there is one lesson that will protect you for the rest of your life, it is this: You are allowed to say no.

No to toxic people.

No to relationships that drain you.

No to anyone who disrespects your boundaries.

You do not owe anyone access to you.

3. Choose Growth Over Familiarity

When you've lived in chaos for so long, peace can feel strange. You might find yourself drawn to familiar patterns, even if they are unhealthy.

Resist that pull.

Familiar does not mean safe. Choose relationships that challenge you to heal, grow, and thrive.

4. Build a Life That Fulfills You

For so long, your world may have revolved around the narcissist. Now, it is time to make yourself the center of your own life.

Find hobbies that light you up.

Travel to places that make you feel free.

Surround yourself with people who uplift and support you.

The best revenge against a narcissist is not hatred—it is indifference and a life well lived.

5. Use Your Story to Empower Others

There is a saying: "Be the person you needed when you were struggling."

Your story matters. Your experience has meaning. And someday, you may be the voice that helps someone else escape the same pain you once endured.

You are not just a survivor. You are a warrior.

Additional Resources for Continued Healing

Your journey doesn't end here. There are many books, therapy options, and communities that can help you continue to heal.

Books for Healing

The Body Keeps the Score – Bessel van der Kolk

Healing from Hidden Abuse – Shannon Thomas

Psychopath Free – Jackson MacKenzie

Online Support Groups

Out of the Fog – Support for survivors of personality-disordered individuals.

Reddit and Facebook Groups – There are many survivor-led communities offering guidance.

Finding the Right Therapist

Look for specialists in narcissistic abuse recovery and trauma therapy.

Websites like BetterHelp and Psychology Today can connect you with professionals.

Final Message

You have walked through fire, but you are still standing.

Healing is not about forgetting—it is about reclaiming your power.

You are not who they said you were. You are who you choose to become.

And the best part?

Your story is just beginning.

Take a deep breath. Hold your head high.

The future is yours.

Appendices

This section is designed to be a practical guide to further your understanding, healing, and growth beyond this book. It includes a glossary of key terms, exercises and journaling prompts for self-reflection, and a comprehensive resource list for continued learning and support.

Glossary of Terms

Understanding the language surrounding narcissistic abuse and healing is essential for empowerment. Below are key terms that have been used throughout this book:

Narcissistic Personality Disorder (NPD)

A mental health condition characterized by grandiosity, a lack of empathy, and a deep need for admiration.

Gaslighting

A psychological manipulation tactic where the narcissist makes you doubt your own memory, perception, or reality to maintain control.

Love Bombing

An early stage in a narcissistic relationship where the narcissist overwhelms their target with excessive affection, compliments, and attention to gain trust and control.

Idealization, Devaluation, Discard Cycle

The cycle of narcissistic abuse that involves:

Idealization – Putting you on a pedestal, treating you as perfect.

Devaluation – Slowly tearing you down, causing confusion and self-doubt.

Discard – Suddenly abandoning or rejecting you, often cruelly.

Hoovering

A manipulation tactic where a narcissist tries to "suck" you back into the relationship after a breakup, often with fake apologies or false promises.

Triangulation

A method of manipulation where the narcissist brings a third person into the relationship to create jealousy, insecurity, or competition.

Silent Treatment

A form of emotional abuse where the narcissist ignores you to punish or control you.

Grey Rock Method

A detachment strategy where you become as emotionally unresponsive and uninteresting as possible to a narcissist, reducing their ability to manipulate you.

No Contact

The act of completely cutting off communication with the narcissist to protect yourself from further harm.

Cognitive Dissonance

The mental discomfort experienced when you hold conflicting beliefs, such as believing the narcissist loves you while also recognizing their abusive behavior.

Inner Child Work

A healing approach that focuses on reconnecting with and healing past wounds from childhood that may have contributed to patterns of people-pleasing or trauma bonding.

These terms serve as powerful tools for understanding and reclaiming your emotional freedom.

Exercises and Journaling Prompts

Journaling can be a profound way to process your experiences and reframe your mindset. Use the following exercises and prompts to aid in your healing journey:

1. Identifying Red Flags in Past Relationships

Write down moments in past relationships where you felt confused, belittled, or manipulated. What were the warning signs? What did your gut tell you?

2. Reclaiming Your Self-Identity

List five things that the narcissist made you doubt about yourself. Now, write five truths about who you actually are.

3. Setting Boundaries with Confidence

Write a letter to yourself affirming that you have the right to set boundaries. List three boundaries you will enforce moving forward and why they matter.

4. Self-Compassion Letter

Imagine writing to a close friend who has gone through what you have. What words of kindness and encouragement would you give them? Now, read it back to yourself—you deserve the same love and compassion.

5. Visualizing Your Healing Future

Where do you see yourself in one year? What does healing look like for you? Write about your dream life, free from toxic influences.

Journaling is not just about writing—it is about reconnecting with yourself and creating the life you deserve.

Comprehensive Resource List

Your healing does not stop here. Below are recommended books, online support groups, and therapy resources to help you on your journey:

Books on Narcissistic Abuse and Recovery

The Body Keeps the Score – Bessel van der Kolk

Healing from Hidden Abuse – Shannon Thomas

Psychopath Free – Jackson MacKenzie

Whole Again – Jackson MacKenzie

Dodging Energy Vampires – Dr. Christiane Northrup

Final Note

Healing is a lifelong journey, not a race. You are not alone, and you never have to go back to the person who broke you.

Keep moving forward. Keep choosing yourself.

The best is yet to come.

www.ingramcontent.com/pod-product-compliance
Lightning Source LLC
LaVergne TN
LVHW012025060526
838201LV00061B/4461